U.S.F. Constellation: "Yankee Racehorse"

By
Sanford Sternlicht
and
Edwin M. Jameson

© Sanford Sternlicht and U.S.F. Constellation Foundation, Inc., 1981

LIBERTY PUBLISHING COMPANY
Cockeysville, Maryland

Published by:
Liberty Publishing Company, Inc.
50 Scott Adam Road
Cockeysville, Maryland 21030

Library of Congress #81-84998
ISBN 0-89709-030-6

Editor: Lynn W. Stonesifer
Cover: From original oil painting
by Arthur N. Disney, Sr.

Manufactured USA

Contents

Introduction

Today, two American warships bear the name *Constellation*. One is a mammoth aircraft carrier of the mighty Forrestal class, among the largest and most powerful vessels afloat. She is a proud ship, made for attack, displacing over sixty thousand tons and longer than three football fields. In the caverns below decks, her magazines hold nuclear weaponry greater in potential power than all the bombs — nuclear and conventional — expended in World War II. Much of her life and history is before her, as this nation hopes fervently that her awesome strength remains an untested potential.

The other *Constellation* no longer sails on distant seas, showing the flag in far-off ports. She is now moored at a specially-designed pier in the city of Baltimore's Inner Harbor — not far from the site of her original launching on September 7, 1797. Her berth is a meca for thousands of Americans who appreciate our national heritage; after all, she is almost as old as the Republic. Her guns have not been fired in anger since Appomattox and never shall be again, yet she can be as proud as any living ship. *Constellation* deserves honor above most, for she served her country faithfully for 150 years. She is the oldest ship of the United States Navy and is one of the original six frigates commissioned by the Continental Congress. *Constellation* is the first American-designed and American-built warship to win a major victory over an enemy man-of-war.

In the long-forgotten Quasi-War with France (1798-1801), French sailors, amazed at her expert sailing ability and endurance, nicknamed her "Yankee Racehorse." She was fast; she was strong; she was cocky; and, she never lost a battle.

A Navy Is Born

At the end of the Revolutionary War, only one of the thirty-five warships built or purchased by the Continental Congress for action against the British remained in American hands. All the others—together with the ships fitted out by the various states—had been taken by the British Navy or destroyed to prevent their capture. Without a navy to protect them, American merchantmen fell easy prey to the corsairs of the Barbary States and to the men-of-war of European belligerents.

The European war that began after the French Revolution could really be called the "First World War." It was fought in every ocean and on all continents except antarctica. England and France were the major and most tenacious combatants; but the war involved dozens of nations, and it continued until the Treaty of Ghent at the end of 1814 and the final defeat of Napoleon at Waterloo the next year. It was a generation of war.

During the first twenty or so years of American independence, there was little respect on the part of European states for this enormous, but weak, underpopulated, and self-centered nation. Despite the possession of a large and prosperous merchant marine, the United States was powerless as a naval force. How could Great Britain or France, with their squadrons of ships-of-the-line, and fleets of frigates, sloops, and brigs, consider the navy-less nation as any more than a large granary, and her ships any more than handy, floating recruit depots? Even the absurd and anachronistic pirates of Barbary heaped insult, scorn, and derision on the United States; and, as far as the British were concerned, Americans were all without courage. Oh, John Paul Jones had had his moment against *Serapis*, but he was really a pirate, they believed, and like all good American seamen, he was British. Had they not wiped out the American navy during the Revolution, losing only five ships themselves? Had not American captains struck their colors precipitously, burned their own squadrons in shallow water, and even hid below decks during battle? It seemed there was no denying these facts. Yes, the navy a-building in 1797 needed not only ships, but a tradition based on victory.

President Washington's message to Congress in 1790 had called attention to impressment and insult without suggesting a solution to the problems. The treasury of the young Republic was nearly empty, precluding payment of ransom money to the Barbary conscripts. In addition, the leaders of the new nation, every one of whom had had personal experience with the professional military castes of England and France, were as loath to risk the establishment of an armed force in the United States as they would have been to see a monarchy proclaimed in their capital. Of course, the British had lived for over a century with large standing armies and navies without a military take-over.

In 1792, Washington again urged Congress to act. He succeeded in obtaining $40,000, to be paid as ransom for American seamen captured by the Dey of Algiers, and an annual appropriation of $25,000 tribute money for immunity from further attacks. This served merely to stimulate the Dey's ability to wring still more concessions from the United States, and more acts of piracy followed. In the closing months of 1793 alone, eleven American merchantmen were seized in the Mediterranean and more than one hundred American citizens were enslaved in North Africa.

A resolution to equip a navy to protect American commerce

was introduced at the opening of the new Congress in 1794, and it was approved by a small majority. As a result of this resolution, "An Act to provide a Naval Armament" was debated and finally passed by a margin of two votes on March 27. This act gave Secretary of War Henry Knox authority to build the six vessels that were eventually commissioned as the frigates *United States, Constellation, Constitution, President, Congress,* and *Chesapeake.* The debate was acrimonious, and a majority in favor of the bill was obtained only after a rider had been attached that provided that the construction of the ships would be halted if peace with Algiers were negotiated before they were completed.

Joshua Humphreys, the brilliant Quaker shipwright from Philadelphia, had definite ideas about how a navy should be built, and he contacted his friend, Secretary of War Knox. Our Navy, Humphreys said, would be inferior to that of any of the European powers for some time to come; thus it would be advisable to built frigates that would more than match double-decked ships in blowing weather and yet outsail them in light winds. He also noted that if it were decided to build double-deckers, ours should overmatch the three-deckers of other navies in rough weather, as well as be able to evade them in calms or light winds. Know listened. He knew that Humphreys had built some of the finest ships to come from American yards.

Frigates had first appeared in the Mediterranean in the sixteenth century as oared vessels, smaller than galleys, which were used principally for dispatch-bearing. In the seventeenth century, the designation referred to a class predicated on the shape of the underwater body, or, as others maintain, certain deck arrangements. The eighteenth-century frigates were ship-rigged men-of-war whose functions were similar to those of modern cruisers; they were classified according to the number of guns they carried on gun and spar decks. Because of their speed, maneuverability, and fighting qualities, frigates were the favorite ships of many famous naval officers including Lord Nelson, who is reported to have said that when he died they would find the word "frigate" engraved on his heart. During World War II, the name was revived to designate a class of small fast ships used primarily in anti-submarine warfare.

If the infant American Navy were going to build frigates, Humphreys felt that they should have keels at least 150 feet long, and their scantlings, or supports, should be as heavy as those usually used in a 74-gun ship-of-the-line. Ships so designed would be able to carry twenty-eight 32-pounders or thirty 24-pounders on the gun deck, and 12-pounders on the spar deck. As such ships would cost a great deal of money, he advised that they be built of the very best material available so that they would last a long time.

Humphreys, writing to Pennsylvania Senator Robert Morris, had offered precise information about the construction of ships for the new navy. He wanted the beams and decks to be made of the best available Carolina pine, even though British shipbuilders despised that wood because of its reputed splintering characteristics. Humphreys wanted live oak for the knees and lower futtocks. Again, the scantlings had to equal those in 74-gun ships-of-the-line. No expense was to be spared in creating superior ships. With a broadside weight above the frigate class and with superior sailing ability and a larger crew, the new American warship was akin in scope to a pocket battleship or a battle cruiser of this century, having the speed of the lighter vessel and some of the fire power of the heavier class.

In other words, what Humphreys proposed was an entirely new type or class of warship which could not be quickly imitated by other navies, and which would give the United States at least a temporary advantage if she were compelled to fight another naval power. That his views were sound was amply proven by the performance of the frigates in the three wars that followed. Humphreys was a man with a revolutionary naval idea.

After the decision had been reached that the six new ships were to be frigates, it was decided that four—which were to be named *Constitution, President, United States,* and *Chesapeake*— would each mount 44 guns. The other two, eventually christened the *Constellation* and the *Congress,* were to carry thirty-six.

The naval architect and historian Howard I. Chapelle has stated that there is no basis for the belief that these men-of-war were built after French designs, as has sometimes been mentioned. It is true that the naval affairs committee of the Continental Congress asked Benjamin Franklin–the Colonies' minister to France during the Revolution–to secure drafts of the latest French frigates, and that the request was forwarded to John Paul Jones on June 1, 1780. If Captain Jones discussed the matter with the Minister of Marine, there is no evidence that anything came of it and no designs are known to have been forwarded. Even if the French had consented to the use of their plans, they would undoubtedly have been outdated in 1794, and there is no record of British men-of-war mistaking the American-designed frigates for French warships. Although the source of his ideas is unknown, there seems no doubt that Joshua Humphreys himself was responsible for the *Constellation's* plans.

Humphreys was awarded the building of the 44-gun *United States*. David Stodder, of Baltimore, was assigned the building of the 36-gun *Constellation*.

U.S.F. Constellation - *Built in 1797*
From the painting by Antoine Roux, Sen., 1826

As the United States was obliged to build a navy from the ground up, the first requisite was to find a group of experienced naval officers to superintend the construction of its ships and assist the Secretary of War in getting the navy organized. The list of captains who had held naval commissions during the Revolution was scrutinized, and those available were contacted. In early June, the appointments of John Barry, Samuel Nicholson, Silas Talbot, Joshua Barney, Richard Dale, and Thomas Truxtun to be captains in the United States Navy were announced. All but Truxtun, who had commanded privateers in the War for Independence, had served in the Continental Navy.

The First Designated American Fleet

WARSHIP	GUNS	BUILDER	WHERE BUILT	SUPERINTENDENT
United States	44	Joshua Humphreys	Philadelphia	John Barry
Constitution	44	George Claghorn	Boston	Samuel Nicholson
President	44	Forman Cheesman	New York	Silas Talbot
Constellation	38	David Stodder	Baltimore	Thomas Truxtun
Chesapeake	38	John Morgan	Norfolk	Richard Dale
Congress	38	James Hackett	Portsmouth	Joshua Barney

(Originally called 36's, the last three frigates were finally and more realistically rated as 38-gunners.)

President Washington insisted that the benefits accrued from the building of the new ships should be distributed among the various states. After some discussion, the construction of a frigate, whose plans were still identified by a letter of the alphabet, was assigned to each of the seaports of Philadelphia, Boston, New York, Norfolk, Baltimore, and Portsmouth, New Hampshire, and each of the newly commissioned captains was ordered to superintend the work on the ship that he would afterwards command. Thomas Truxtun, who had lately published *Remarks, Instructions, and Examples Relating to the Latitude and Longitude, to which is Annexed Cap't Truxtun's System of Masting,* was given the task of overseeing the construction of the 36-gun Frigate "E" which was to be built at Baltimore.

This was indeed a brilliant stroke on the part of the government. After all, Truxtun had not been an officer in the Continental Navy, but a successful privateer and a merchant captain. The regular Navy officers looked down with scorn upon the ex-privateers, who had served for money and not primarily for patriotism. The regulars conveniently forgot that while the Continental Navy had been swept from the high seas, the privateers had wreaked havoc with British shipping, tied up squadrons of British cruisers, and thus permitted the French fleet to obtain tactical superiority and complete mobility on the east coast of America. The privateers were the submarines of the age of sail. Then, as now, the raiding of commerce was a noose that could strangle a mercantile nation without invasion.

Thomas Truxtun was born in the Town of Hempstead, Long Island, on February 17, 1755, the son of an English barrister. Schooled in Latin, Greek, and mathematics, Truxtun was an orphan at ten, and an apprentice seaman at twelve, shipping out of the teeming ports of Brooklyn and New York. On shore leave in London early in 1771, the sixteen-year-old lad was jumped by a vicious press gang, and, even though carrying merchant protection papers, was abducted into the Royal Navy. He served before the mast in HMS *Prudent,* a 64-gun ship-of-the-line, for several months until discharged after a temporary cessation of European hostilities. Truxtun never forgot this tour of duty under the Union Jack. He was much impressed with the discipline and efficiency of the British Navy, and he must have learned how very important it is for fighting men to expect and believe that they will win. The Royal Navy considered themselves superior man for man, ship for ship, gun crew for gun crew, to anything afloat. It had been proved time and time again in combat. But, to the great chagrin of the Admiralty and the British public, in the

War of 1812, the Americans would emerge victors in evenly matched ships' contests, for, by then America had had Truxtun.

At twenty, Truxtun was skipper of the merchant sloop *Charming Polly*, out of New York and in the West Indies trade. In 1775, the 28-gun British sloop-of-war *Argo* stopped and seized *Charming Polly*, as the Colonies were in a state of rebellion. American ships were now being confiscated everywhere, and the newly-formed Continental Congress decided that two could play the game. Soon Congress and captains like Truxtun were in the privateering business. Truxtun, angry because much of his own money had been tied up in *Charming Polly*, shipped as a prize master, who would sail captured vessels into friendly ports on the 6-gun sloop, *Congress*, one of the first two privateers chartered by Congress.

The first cruise of *Congress* was a success, and soon Truxtun commanded the 10-gun privateer *Independence*. Successful again with *Independence*, Truxtun wanted a more powerful ship for bigger game, and in May, 1777, he commanded the 22-gun *Mars*, with 150 men. This time he sailed in a veritable warship and he made a small fortune. Returning to the merchant service, he lost one ship to the British and nearly lost his second to a Cape Hatteras storm. In his next ship, he bravely and skillfully fought off a well-armed British privateer. After the war, and in command of *London Packet*, Truxtun brought Benjamin Franklin back to the United States from his successful ministry in France. Then, in 1784, he entered the newly commenced China trade, and his *London Packet* was refitted and strengthened in Philadelphia, by Joshua Humphreys. Her new name: *Canton.*

When Congress began contemplating a real navy to protect commerce from Barbary, scores of requests for commissions and commands in the service were received by the War Department. Many applicants were highly qualified; many were not. There is no record that Truxtun actually applied for a command in the Navy, although surely he must have at least expressed interest in serving his country as a naval officer. When the list of captains for the first American squadron was released, there were five former Continental Navy officers on

it, and one civilian, Thomas Truxtun, known throughout the
Eastern Seaboard for his courage, his integrity, and great
navigational ability. The list was ranked for seniority as
follows:

> John Barry
> Samuel Nicholson
> Silas Talbot
> Joshua Barney
> Richard Dale
> Thomas Truxtun

Truxtun, obviously, did not accept the command for the
money involved. His pay was to be seventy-five dollars per
month and six rations: total value under $120. But the chance
for service and glory—ah there were things worth far more
than gold or goods!

Barney, having decided he should have been senior to Talbot, huffed off to join the French Navy, thus moving all up
one notch. Truxtun now had the choice of a 36-gun at Portsmouth, New Hampshire, or one at Baltimore. He chose Baltimore, and set out to find a shipyard. He rejected the many
yards at Fell's Point, and instead chose the yard of the naval
constructor, David Stodder.

Meanwhile, with senior officers appointed and locations decided upon for the building of its new warships, the government's next problem was to obtain suitable materials with
which to get the actual construction under way. The procure-
ment of live oak timber–which Humphreys had specified for
the principal frames of the frigates because of its toughness
and durability–proved to be particularly difficult. A supply of
well-seasoned logs that had been cut for two 74-gun ships in
1776 was located near the mouth of the Savannah River in
Georgia. But the work of cutting them to the molds or pat-
terns sent down by Humphreys and getting them to the ship-
yards was plagued by accidents, fever, and shipwreck. The
grade of heart pitch pine that Humphreys wished to use for
deck beams and the lower decks proved to be scarce in the
dimensions required, and, at Truxtun's insistence, the substitution of white oak was finally permitted for the beams. As
the supply of copper was limited in the United States, an

order for approximately twenty-seven tons of copper sheathing, bolts, and nails was placed with the London firm of Alexander Bisland and Company.

. But it was wood, wood, wood that plagued the shipbuilders
up and down the coast. How ironic—a nation of trees, a continent of trees, and yet magnificently designed American
vessels fell apart after just a few years in salt water. Wood
had to be skillfully dried and cured, and all too often American shipbuilders were unable to invest the time and money in
these processes. Also, transportation out of the forests–such
as the Catskills or the live oak forests of coastal South Carolina and Georgia–was almost non-existent for freight as
heavy and bulky as ship's timbers. Ultimately, Truxtun,
somewhat out of his element–led safaris of axe-men into the
hinterlands to cut many of his own timbers for the Frigate
"E". Imagine, a naval commander who would know every
peg, every nail, every beam, of his ship! Surely Truxtun was
beginning to love the growing wood pile, as yet only a ship's
shadow, as one loves the child he nurtures.

Suddenly, there is peace with Algiers and the building of
the Navy is aborted before it ever gets underway. In accordance with the provisions of the Act of 1794, all work on the
frigates is stopped.

Still not convinced of the futility of trying to appease the
appetites of a ruler who had a superior military force, the
United States agreed to pay a tribute of nearly one million
dollars (including a fully equipped frigate worth approximately one hundred thousand dollars) to the Dey, and promised an
annual gift of $21,600 in naval stores. President Washington
felt strongly that the Congress was making a mistake in
agreeing to the treaty unless it also made provision for a
Navy to enforce it.

As a result of the President's message calling attention to
the provisions of the Act of 1794, the Chairman of the Committee of the House of Representatives (concerned with the
building of the frigates) pointed out that much money would
be lost if the work on the frigates were suddenly discontinued. He asked the Secretary of War to report on their progress. In a reply dated January 20, 1796, the Secretary gave

an estimate of the final cost of the ships and expressed the opinion that they could be "built, launched, and completely equipt" in 1796.
launched, and completely equipt" in 1796.

This information was transmitted to Congress and on April 20, 1796, "An Act to provide a naval Armament" was passed. This authorized the President to proceed with the construction and equipment of the two 44-gun and the 36-gun frigate on which work was farthest advanced. A survey revealed that these ships would be the ones afterwards known as the 44-gun *United States,* the 44-gun *Constitution,* and the 36-gun *Constellation.*

President Washington made a final plea for a Navy in his last message to Congress on December 7, 1796, when he said:

To an active external commerce, the protection of a naval force is indispensable. This is manifest with regard to wars, in which a state is itself a party. But, besides this, it is in our own experience, that the most sincere neutrality is not a sufficient guard against the depredations of nations at war. To secure respect to a neutral flag, requires a naval force, organized, and ready to vindicate it from insult or aggression. This may even prevent the necessity of going to war, by discouraging belligerent powers from committing such violations of the rights of the neutral party, as may, first or last, leave us no other option. From the best information I have been able to obtain, it would seem as if our trade to the Mediterranean, without a protecting force, will always be insecure, and our citizens exposed to the calamities from which numbers of them have just been relieved.

These considerations invite the United States to look to the means, and to set about the gradual creation of a Navy. The increasing progress of their navigation promises them, at no distant period, the requisite supply of seamen; and their means, in other respects, favor the undertaking. It is an encouragement, likewise, that their particular situation will give weight and influence to a moderate naval force in their hands. Will it not then be advisable to begin, without delay, to provide and lay up materials for the building and equipping of ships of war; and to proceed in the work, by degrees, in proportion, as our resources shall render it practicable, without inconvenience; so that a future war of Europe may not find our commerce in the same unprotected state, in which it was found by the present.

As definite orders to stop work on the frigates had never been issued by the President, the collection of materials for the *Constellation* continued through the winter of 1795-96. On February 5, 1796, the ceremony of "raising" her stern post took place and the outlines of her hull gradually became visible. As soon as Captain Truxtun received word in April that his frigate was among those to be finished, the work was pushed with renewed vigor "to have her speedily compleated, and in a way that will do honor to the United States."

In the meantime, President Washington had selected the names for the proposed ships, and it was announced that the Frigate "E" would be christened *Constellation*—named for a new group of bright stars, each a state in the Union and together a symbol of hope and freedom.

William Rush, a Philadelphia wood-carver who was especially celebrated for his work on ships, was commissioned to execute the decorations for the *Constellation* and the *United States*. Rush suggested that the figurehead for the former should be represented by: "An elegant female figure, characteristic of indignant Nature, at the period of the American Revolution determined on forming a New Creation, from that Chaos of Ignorance, Vice and Folly, which she had long been burthened with . . . She should have a flaming torch in her right hand, setting fire to the bursting world under her feet, with the emblems of Tyranny Superstition Folly, & issuing from it, and thrown into Confusion and fermentation, her left arm resting on the altar of Liberty. The American eagle in the act of flight, a Sphere resting on his pinions with the Constellation inserted."

By the summer of 1797, the work on the frigate's hull was well advanced, with the planking completed and the workmen beginning to copper-sheath the portion below the waterline. The decks and interior structures were progressing satisfactorily, although there was still some delay in getting delivery of the materials required. The prospect of getting her ready for launching before cold weather appeared good.

The 44-gun *United States* was the first of the new frigates to be launched; but a great inclination of the ways resulted in her sliding into the Delaware River before all the keel blocks had been removed, and some of her underwater planking was damaged. Hoping to avoid a similar accident to the Baltimore frigate, the War Department ordered Joshua Humphreys to go to that city to "consult on the best Method to be pursued in launching the Frigate *Constellation* in the Water (so as to float)." By the middle of August, it was apparent that the *Constellation* would be ready early in the following month.

The ship was indeed a thing of beauty. The smallest of the three frigates whose completion had been authorized, her long narrow lines and the pronounced tumble-home of her sides—that were so characteristic of Humphrey's designs— gave promise of the speed that would win her the nickname of the "Yankee Racehorse." A sea captain in the crowd shook his head after a look at the size of her masts and spars that were still piled in the yard and predicted that she would be topheavy. Her greyhound-lean shape, however, would become a characteristic of the later Baltimore Clippers.

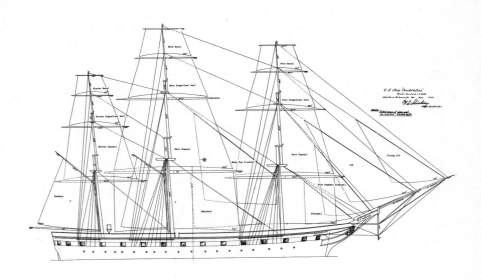

U.S.F. Constellation
Truxtun's Spar and Rigging Plan

What were the new vessel's dimensions? The length on deck measured 171 feet and she was forty feet in the beam. She drew twenty feet of water, displacing roughly 1,265 tons. The high main mast towered 150 feet above the deck, including the topmast, topgallant, and royal, with another seventeen feet stepped into the hold.

The dull black of *Constellation*'s hull, relieved only by a white stripe at the level of the gun deck ports, set off the bright colors of her figurehead and stern carvings. The stern was decorated with a large sphere "with the Constellation inserted, resting on a mossy pedestal." One side of the pedestal was decorated with the fasces, three large volumes, and a scroll, representing the three branches of the government and the constitution, while the other side bore an eagle and a shield. On the starboard side of the transom, Fortitude was depicted with the symbols of Order, Industry, and Agriculture, "supported by Ceres, the goddess of agriculture," while the port quarter-piece carried the figure of Justice with the emblems of Science, Shipbuilding, and Navigation "supported by Neptune, the god of the seas."

Captain Truxtun climbed the ramp and went aboard the frigate, passing through a gangway in the bulwarks. It was decorated on each side with an instained mahogany panel on which were carved an eagle perched on a globe, acanthus scrolls, and a shield flanked with three flags and containing a single star. The decks were still littered with lumber and shavings, but the mahogany steering wheel and the capstan were in place. Three circular holes to receive the masts had been cut in the deck and some of the skylights had been installed, but the hatches were still without their gratings and the long amidship hatch remained open to the sky.

Visitors, descending a ladder to the gun deck, were impressed with the massiveness of the curved white oak knees and beams. They saw that the sides of the frigate were pierced for fourteen long 24-pounder guns on each side. The after portion of this deck was partitioned off to form the captain's cabin. There was a tiny lead-seated toilet and a lead bathtub in the quarter gallery on the port side and another to starboard. Between these small cabins was a private cabin for the captain, and farther forward was a larger cabin which served as a chartroom and library, as well as a dining room.

The deck below the gun deck contained the officers' wardroom, which was located aft under the captain's cabin, and the berthing spaces for the crew. While examining this deck, the visitor had to stoop to avoid knocking his head against the same type of heavy beams and knees that he had seen on the gun deck, for the 'tween deck height was less than six feet.

The wardroom, not yet finished, was fitted with tiny state rooms on each side that were separated from the common room by partitions balustraded in their upper half to provide ventilation. Aft of the wardroom was a narrow space containing the tiller, where junior officers might be permitted to sling their hammocks if the wardroom were overcrowded. The entire deck from the "officers' country" forward to the bow was left clear for the hammocks of the petty officers and crew. Still deeper in the frigate's interior were the orlop deck, where the midshipmen had their living quarters, the magazine and shot rooms, and spaces for stowing fresh water casks and ballast.

"Wind, weather, and tide permitting," announced the *Baltimore Telegraph*, "the United States Frigate *Constellation*, will be launched on Thursday, the 7th of September." Hundreds of spectators had come out from the city to witness the gala event. The Army Commander of the Fort on Whetstone Point (later called Fort McHenry), who had given twelve of his few cannon to help arm the new ship, provided guards for the launch. The soldiers wore dress uniforms, naval personnel wore their finest gear, and the ladies and civilian gentlemen wore Sunday best.

Truxtun looked over the rail nervously, thinking of Humphreys, whose last launch had damaged the ship concerned, but when he saw the busy Mr. Stodder, his worries ceased. With the flood tide, Stodder gave the order to raise the hull a few inches with wedges until the keel blocks were cleared away and the weight moved onto the bilge ways made fast to the hull. The launch ways had been thoroughly lubricated with barrels of tallow. Using a drum to telegraph his commands, Stodder ordered all men out from the ways and signaled for a burly yard worker to knock out the last holding stanchion. For a moment nothing happened. The crowd hushed. Then slowly, and accompanied by a crescendo of shrieking timbers, the *Constellation* slid with increasing speed and momentum to her natural element. The cheers were deafening. The launching was perfect. Stodder followed the anchoring of the ship with an almost sad eye. She was Truxtun's now.

Joshua Humphreys was unable to attend the launch. That afternoon Truxtun wrote to his old friend describing the event:

At 9 A.M. the Frigate Constellation was Safely launched — A Better Launch I never Saw; the Ship Cleared the ways, without touching or Meeting with the Smallest Accident — in fact every precaution to Guard Against Accident, Stodder tooke, and for the Manner he Secured, and laid the Ways, I cannot but give him, the highest Credit as a Master Builder etc. — Tomorrow I shall erect the Sheers, and on Saturday take in the Mizzen Mast . . . . P.S. The Ship did not Strain in the least, or Straiten her Sheer —"

Thomas Truxtun (1755-1822)

Ready To Sail

Captain Truxtun had planned on taking the *Constellation* to the Patuxent River, where the work of fitting out could be continued without having to worry about the ice that usually formed in the Patapsco. However, an epidemic of yellow fever in Baltimore caused a change of plan. Within three days of the launching it was reported that the bodies of a dozen victims of the dread "yellow jack" were being removed from the vicinity of the shipyard every night. Work on the frigate came to an abrupt standstill, and it was not until October that the masts could be stepped and the rigging placed. Hundreds of items of equipment required to make the ship ready for sea had to be checked and carried on board, but the river froze and the work had to be discontinued until spring.

Meanwhile, Europe was seething with the struggles arising from the French Revolution, and the United States found herself in the unhappy position of a neutral whose neutrality was respected by none of the belligerents. During and immediately following the overthrow of the monarchy in France, American public opinion favored the French cause, and pro-French demonstrations in Philadelphia and New York irritated England. In addition, the activities of Citizen Genet –who had been appointed French minister to the United

States in 1793-soon proved so embarrassing that American sympathies were alienated, and Secretary of State Thomas Jefferson requested Genet's recall. As the United States had no military or naval forces with which to enforce her neutrality, England, France, and Spain seized American merchantmen, whether or not they carried contraband of war or were within the territorial waters of this country. They were protected by the knowledge that they had nothing other to fear than a diplomatic protest.

As the relations between the United States and England were still tinged with bitterness, John Jay was sent to London in 1794 as a Minister Extraordinary to try to arrange a treaty of "amity, commerce, and navigation." This was ratified on October 28, 1795, and Great Britain agreed to stop interfering with American commerce and to compensate the owners of the vessels and cargoes that had already been captured. Unfortunately, as events in 1812 were to prove, Jay could not persuade England to end her warships' practice of stopping American ships and impressing their seamen into her service. One English captain, after boarding an American merchantman and taking off several of the protesting crew, scorned their declaration of American citizenship, writing in his diary that they must have been British because "they spoke English exceedingly well."

Jay's treaty with Great Britain displeased France and led her to renew her complaints that the United States was not living up to the terms of her 1778 agreements. While diplomatic negotiations were under way between the two countries, French privateers continued to harass American commerce, especially in the West Indies. In January, 1797, the *Veritude,* a French privateer, entered the harbor of Charleston, South Carolina, and captured the English ship *Oracabissa,* which she then burned. Proceeding to sea on the following day, the *Veritude* added insult to injury by capturing the American ship *Pallas,* of Charleston, and the brig *Mary,* of Savannah, both well within the territorial waters of the United States. To strain France's relations with the United States still further, three commissioners were sent to Paris in October, 1797, to negotiate a treaty with the Directory, similar to the Jay treaty with England. Their efforts came to naught.

Such repeated insults to the nation's honor raised President Adams' Yankee blood to the boiling point. Without waiting for Congressional approval, he issued orders for Captain Truxtun to prepare his ship for active service and to recruit a crew.

When Congress met in the spring and was told of the cavalier treatment that the President's mission had received from the French Directory and of the depredations of French privateers in American waters, a series of defensive measures was passed with little debate. On March 27, 1798, a bill was passed appropriating $115,833 to complete the frigates *United States, Constitution,* and *Constellation* and equip them for sea. On April 30, another act established a Navy Department with Benjamin F. Stoddert of Georgetown, D.C., as the first Secretary. On May 28, "An Act more effectually to protect the commerce and coasts of the United States" was enacted. It was implemented a few days later by President Adams' instructions to the commanders of the nation's armed vessels:

Whereas, it is declared by an act of Congress passed the 28th day of May, 1798, that armed vessels sailing under authority or pretence of authority, from the French Republic, have committed depredations on the commerce of the United States, and have recently captured the vessels and property of citizens thereof, on and near the coasts, and in violation of the law of nations, and treaties between the United States and the French nation:—

Therefore, and in pursuance of the said act, you are instructed and directed to seize, take, and bring into any port of the United States, any armed vessels sailing under authority or pretence of authority from the Republic of France, which shall have committed, or which shall be found hovering on the coast of the United States for the purpose of committing depredations on the vessels belonging to the citizens thereof; and also to retake any ship or vessel of any citizen or citizens of the United States, which have been captured by any such armed vessel.

Such were the events leading up to the Quasi-War with France. The contest was initiated without a formal declaration of hostilities by either side; commercial relations between the belligerents were maintained throughout its course; and the personal property of French citizens was scrupulously respected. Whatever its other accomplishments may have been, the undeclared war with France resulted in the organization of the Unted States Navy and gave its ships and the men who commanded them an opportunity to prove their mettle in actual combat.

In the first week of April, 1798, the *Constellation* dropped down Chesapeake Bay to the mouth of the Patuxent River, and Captain Truxtun undertook the task of getting his ship ready for sea. A recruiting station was set up in Baltimore by Lieutenant John Rodgers, who had been ordered to the *Constellation* as Second Lieutenant. After five weeks, fewer than a hundred seamen had been signed on for the frigate's first cruise. The pay of fifteen dollars a month for able seamen and ten dollars a month for ordinary seamen had little appeal to the men of Baltimore; They could earn half as much again on a merchantman, where the discipline was less strict and a man did not have to provide a sea bag full of uniforms. As an added incentive to enlistment in the new Navy, a dollar a month was added to the pay of petty officers and the pay of able seamen was increased to seventeen dollars a month.

To complete the crew, the *Constellation's* Third Lieutenant, Mr. William Cowper, was sent to Norfolk where another hundred hands were signed on. James Triplett, a lieutenant of artillery in the United States Army, was persuaded to accept the temporary billet of Lieutanant of Marines and was sent to Alexandria, where he succeeded in enrolling nearly sixty survivors of a vessel that had been captured by a French privateer. They reported for duty in the marine contingent and as seamen.

With his ship's company finally assembled, Captain Truxtun drew up the watch quarter, and station bills and undertook the task of familiarizing his officers and men with their duties. The rules for the regulation of the Navy, adopted by Congress on July 1, 1797, were elaborated by Truxtun and explained to his crew, and the commissioned and warrant officers were given detailed written instructions on what was required of each.

James Yeomans, master carpenter, was told to "be particularly careful of all the Spars, Boat Oars, Pump Gear, Tools, Pitch, Rosin, Turpentine, Varnish, Paints, Oil, and other

Stores in your Department, and have the same at Hand and ready for Use at all Times. You will see, that every Matter appertaining to your Business, is kept in repair, and report any Defects, that may appear, as soon as it is seen. You are particularly charged with having the Ship well wet Night and Morning, *inside and out.*"

The Armorer, Mr. Bankson, was told that, "Your general duty as Armourer consists in obeying the orders you may receive from time to time from the Commanding Officer on deck. Your particular duty is to take Charge of all tools and apparatus belonging to the department of Armourer and Gun Smith and to assist the gunner in the Survey of all Small Arms and to keep them Clean and in good order. You are further to consider Yourself Under the gunner's direction and to be of his Crew . . . You will also in performing your duty obey the directions of the Lieutenant of Marines and Master of Arms and make Yourself as Useful as possible in Makeing & Repairing all sorts of tools in every department on Board."

After admonishing the Boatswain, Abraham Long, to be attentive to the rigging, anchors, cables, blocks and other boatswain's stores for which he was responsible, Truxtun informed him that he was subject to the orders of the sea lieutenants and sailing master. "It is your duty under Such orders as may be issued to direct whatever relates to the Rigging, to observe the Masts are properly supported by their Shrouds, Stays and backe stays. So that each may sustain a proportional effort when the Masts are strained by the violence of the wind, or the agitation of the Ship . . . You are to take care that the blocks and running ropes are regularly placed, So as to answer the purpose intended, & you are also to take care that the sails are properly fitted, kept in repair handsomely and Securely bent, well furled and reefed when orders are issued for the latter purpose . . . It is your duty to Summon the Crew to theirs to assist in the neccesary business of the Ship, and to relieve the watch when it expires, to examine the Condition of the Masts, Sails and Rigging; remove what is unfit for Service and Supply what is deficient, and to perform this duty with as little noise as possible . . . Your Mates are to assist you, in all the functions of your office; they are to be vigilant in turning up the Watch or all hands as occasion may require; they as well as yourself are to carry and wind a call. Compel a manly exertion in the Crew on all occasions, and to punish (as orders may be given) where it is deemed Necessary — You will keep a regular account of all articles received and expended. Attend Minutely to the rules and regulations issued by the President of the United States, through the Department of the Navy and with those of your Crew, have every article in your department kept in good order and at hand and to direct your Yeoman, not to suffer any of the store apparatus under your Charge to be left lying about the decks or otherwise kept out of place but to keep An Account of all Stores received and expended."

James Morgan, Gunner, was to consider himself in charge of the "Artillery and Ammunition recd on board, and such as may hereafter be received you are to observe that the Cannon are always kept in order, and properly fitted with tackles and other furniture, and to instruct the Seamen etc in the use and management of them. You are to keep the Cannon well tompioned and putty'd and have everything prepared agreeable to the instructions I have, and may hereafter issue, so that in a few minutes warning the ship may be ready at any time to go into an Engagement by night or day—The Gunner's Mate and his Yeoman, are to assist you in every part of your duties they should be as well acquainted with Gunnery and everything respecting the ordinance and Military Stores as the Gunner himself, their particular business under the Gunner, is to have everything ready for action in a moment's warning, they should never be at a loss where to lay their hands upon any article belonging to the Gunner's department; they should be expert in preparing to Match Stuff, Grenadoes, and every sort of Combustible and in a word, in doing every part of a Gunner's duty on board a Ship of War.—The Quarter Gunners are to assist in every part of this duty, as keeping the Guns and their Carriages in [illegible] order and duly furnished with whatever is necessary, filling powder into Cartridges, Scaling the Guns, and keeping them always in a condition for Service—You will hence-forward be particular in attending to your duty and causing all under you to do the same—The Stowage of the Magazine, StoreRoom, [illegible] Care and distribution of all the Stores in your department should be Minutely attended to."

The Master at Arms, John Marshall, was told to "exercise the Crew and teach them the use of Small Arms—To Confine and plant Centinels over the prisoners, and Superintend whatever relates to them during their Confinement—You are to see all lights and fire extinguished according to regulations except Such as shall be permitted by proper Authority, or under the inspection of Centinels . . . It is likewise your duty to attend the Gangway, when any boates arrive along Side, and Search them Carefully, together with their rowers, that no Spiritous liquors may be conveyed into the Ship—You are to See that the Small Arms are kept in proper order, to visit all vessels comeing to, or going from the ship without leave—You are to Acquaint the Officers of the watch with all irregularities in the Ship, which Shall come to your Knowledge—In these several duties You are to be assisted by the Corporals, who relieve one Another at proper periods."

While still at anchor in the Patuxent River an order was issued establishing four watches:

First and Second Watches: 2 midshipmen
1 Master's mate
1 Quartermaster
1 Boatswain's mate

Third Watch: 2 midshipmen
1 Master's mate
1 Quartermaster
1 Carpenter's mate

Fourth Watch: 2 midshipmen
1 Coxswain
1 Quartermaster
1 Carpenter's mate

All watches also included thirty Seamen and ordinary seamen and boys.

The Gunner was also given minute directions on arming the tops, and the Purser was directed to deliver the hospital stores to Dr. Balfour as requested. Lieutenant of Marines James Triplett had his duties explained, and letters had to be sent to the Secretary of War explaining the receipt of more lanterns than ordered and the loss of a small bower anchor when the ring gave way.

In his letter to the Secretary, Truxtun noted that the *Constellation's* draft exceeded twenty-two feet, which made it impossible for her to enter any port in the U.S. south of the Chesapeake without taking out her guns. In connection with the loss of his anchor he referred to many previous complaints about their poor quality and said that he would not have accepted the ones given the *Constellation* in Baltimore if others had been available. "Suitable Anchors should be provided for all sorts of Ships, but particularly for heavy Vessels, I have never seen any made in this Country fit for a Frigate."

By May 28, when President Adams issued his instructions to the commanders of United States' armed vessels, Captain Truxtun had an organization that was ready to go to sea and prove that the United States at long last had a Navy.

On May 30, the *Constellation* received orders to put to sea and cruise from Cape Henry to the "extremity of the southern limits" of the United States, then considered to be the St. Mary's River in Georgia. Captain Richard Dale in the 24-gun *Ganges,* would patrol from Long Island to Cape Henry.

The first three weeks of June were filled with activity as *Constellation* made her way from the Patuxent to Hampton Roads. The innumerable details of getting the ship "in all respects" ready for sea received the personal attention of the Captain, and his yeoman was kept busy with the correspondence.

In early June, orders were received that the *Constellation* and the 20-gun *Delaware,* which was under the command of Captain Stephen Decatur, Sr., were to put to sea in search of French privateers operating between Cape Henry and the southern limits of the United States. While awaiting the arrival of a group of merchantmen that he had agreed to convoy beyond the Capes, Truxtun filled his water casks, took the last of his stores aboard, and scaled his new guns by firing a few charges of powder. At noon on June 26, the *Constellation* hoisted the signal for her convoy to get under way and in the late afternoon passed Cape Henry on her starboard beam with her course shaped for the southeastward.

The chunky 43-year-old captain who paced the weather side of the *Constellation's* quarterdeck on her first cruise was no novice who owed his position to political favoritism, but a professional sailor who had spent most of the last thirty-one years of his life at sea. The one-time victim of a London press gang was thoroughly familiar with the traditions that had made the Royal Navy pre-eminent in the eighteenth century, and he was convinced that the young United States Navy could profit by emulating the ideals and many of the methods of the British service.

A theorist as well as a practical seaman, Truxtun appreciated the necessity of an over-all organization that would weld the new Navy into a unit. His *Remarks, Instructions, and Examples Relating to the Latitude and Longitude, to which is Annexed Cap't Truxtun's System of Masting*, which was published in 1794, was the first book on the subject to be written by an American. This treatise, which deals with many more matters than its title suggests, contains a chapter on the duties of the individual officers of a man-of-war and was written while the question of building a navy for the United States was still under discussion in Congress, long before its author had any thought of entering her service. Truxtun's second book, *Instructions, Signals, and Explanations offered for the U.S. Fleet*, was written in his spare time while his frigate was under construction, and was published at Baltimore in 1797. In this compilation, which was taken in large part from Royal Navy sources, he attempts to set up a code of flag, sound, and light signals that would enable ships to communicate or identify each other under the conditions of daylight, fog, or darkness.

It would have been easy to predict that, under such a commander, the *Constellation* was going to sea with a disciplined and well organized crew and a staff of officers who knew what their captain expected of them. The drills that would forge them into a fighting team would come later.

Truxtun's explicit orders to his officers, which usually ended with the warning that if they wanted to get along on the frigate they had better carry out their duties exactly as ordered, appear to have had the desired effect in general although there is evidence to the contrary concerning Lieutenant Triplett and his Marines. On June 25, Truxtun sent a memo to the lieutenants and master of the frigate advising them that the Marines had been directed to "pull, hawl, and heave at the Capstern, in Addition to the Duty assigned them under the Lieutenant of Marines." At the same time he expressed his displeasure at the Marines' carelessness and neglect in the care and cleanliness of their clothing. And finally, he reminded Lieutenant Triplett that the Marines were to be exercised and paraded at sunrise and sunset when in port, though they need not be mustered until seven A.M. when at sea. At general quarters and when the guns were exercised, they were to take part in the drills ordered.

A few days after leaving Hampton Roads, Truxtun sensed that trouble was brewing in the forward part of the ship. For reasons of his own and with the authority of the Navy behind him, he had given orders that the daily allowance of water was to be limited to two quarts a day which was to be issued a pint at a time. The crew saw no necessity for such rationing and felt that it was just another example of the strict discipline to which they had been subjected since they had come on board.

Never one to dilly-dally when faced with such a problem, Truxtun had the men mustered at the main mast and read the Articles of War. After pointing out that their actions of the past few days were not far from mutinous, he cited the Articles dealing with such behavior, and, after assuring them that he was fully prepared to carry out the provisions of the Articles to the letter if necessary, warned them to be more attentive in the future.

To prove that he meant business when he said that he intended to have a disciplined ship, he ordered a marine triced up to a grating and flogged "with one Dozen of Stripes on his bare Back, with a Cat of nine Tails, for Insolence to the Sergeant of Marines, and endeavoring to arest a Pistol out of his Hands." This was the only time on record that Captain Truxtun resorted to such punishment.

At Truxtun's command, the boatswain's mate of the watch piped "all hands on deck" in the shrill notes of his instrument. Then he shouted down the main hatch, "All hands witness punishment." His mates below took up the cry and passed it along. Swiftly, the barefooted crew moved topside. The divisions formed to port and starboard on the spar deck in long lines. The marines stood straight as spears, while the sailors fidgeted nervously. The captain spoke with determination to the First Lieutenant: "You may proceed, sir."

Lieutenant Gross called; "Master at Arms, bring forth the prisoner!"

The marine was marched forward, and lashed to the up-ended deck grating. He never flinched, either before or during punishment. His very manhood was at stake. He was being judged by his peers and must not be found wanting in courage if he was to keep face in the small world of a ship's forecastle.

The boatswain's mate took the cat from the bag. It was a short wooden club, with nine ropes attached, each ending with a lead pellet to cut deeply into the flesh of the back.

"Do your duty. Give him one dozen and lay them on with a will," Truxtun spoke without malice.

The mate raised his muscled arm and the cat whistled fiercely through the air. The marine's body shuddered as if shot and nine welts sprang up between his shoulder blades. Another blow, and blood began to drip from crosses in the flesh. After the twelfth, the silent marine, his sweat running into his wounds was then cut down and taken below, his jacket lightly thrown over his shoulders. The surgeon would minister to him, perhaps by rubbing salt as an antiseptic into his wounds. Men listened, but there was not a cry from sickbay.

The brutality of flogging was long recognized by Truxtun's time and the American Navy used it sparingly, allowing captains the authority to award only twelve lashes to a man for each offense. In the Royal Navy men were regularly flogged "around the fleet," receiving hundreds of lashes and whipped even when dead, their bodies looking more like scorched meat than human flesh.

Despite the Constitution's prohibition against cruel and unusual punishment, American seamen were flogged until the punishment was abolished by Congress in 1852, thanks to the efforts of Commodore Uriah Phillips Levy and Senator Richard Stockton of New Jersey, a former naval officer. In the Royal Navy, captains were prohibited by an Act of Parliament in 1866, from awarding more than forty-eight lashes at a time. It was not until 1879, that the British abolished flogging. Other cruel punishments arose, however, in both services including "tricing up," hanging a man by his wrists for hours with his toes barely touching the deck.

Interestingly, it was the sailors themselves who resisted the abolishment of the barbaric punishment of flogging, feeling that the elimination of the threat of corporal punishment would ruin Navy discipline and make life harder for the obedient sailor. Furthermore, many sailors did not think flogging to be degrading, but rather accepted it as a challenge to their manhood. One old tar in a man-of-war was brought to Captain's mast for drunkeness and fighting. The skipper said in disgust: "You are a disgrace to the ship. You deserve a dozen lashes but out of respect for your age I'm awarding you two days' extra duty and restriction to the ship for a month."

Shocked, the old man ripped off his shirt, showing a calloused and crisscrossed back, hard from many a lashing. "Don't say thet, sar, I'm not ta auld to stand up and take me floggin' like a man!" Restriction and extra duty were boys' punishments. The cat was for men. Only loss of a grog ration was "cruel and unusual punishment" for a Yankee tar.

All Hands On Deck

Of just two things could a man be sure when he boarded the frigate on which he had enlisted: he was going to be crowded and before the cruise was over he would probably be bored. Both officers and weather were unpredictable and the cruise could be packed with high adventure, or be so uneventful that when he looked back there was scarcely a day that differed from the one before it and the one that followed. The routine of his waking hours would follow a pattern varied only by coming to anchor, getting under way, or actual contact with an enemy. Otherwise, the days of his life rolled on like the interminable waves: each one like the last until, one day, almost suddenly, he awoke old and dry and there were no more watches left.

The Boatswain and his mates would rouse him out at dawn if the ship was in port, or in time to get on deck before his watch, if at sea. At 6 bells in the second dogwatch each evening, he would have to sling his hammock on a berth deck where the overhead was so low that it was impossible to stand upright, and where the space allotted each man measured only twenty-two inches wide by eight feet long.

On coming aboard his new ship the old-timer would be likely to find a number of former shipmates who would try to outdo one another in helping him to get settled. One might take his seabag to the bagroom, another would sling a clean hammock for him or stow it in the netting, while a third would introduce him to his new messmates. The apprentice seaman, not having had the advantage of the modern "boot" training, would find himself a veritable "wanderer in a foreign land, ignorant alike of the language or manners of the inhabitants, bashful of obtruding his notice upon anyone, fearing a rebuke, and becoming inadvertently the butt of every shallow-pated, self-sufficient ignoramus who chose to level his insults upon him."

One foretopman, recalling his own introduction to the Navy, wrote, "as I daily beheld the entrance of your *saplings,* aspirants for naval enterprise, I felt pity for their inexperience and loneliness, and bearing in mind how I myself was situated in a former similar occasion, I cultivated the acquaintance of each, putting them on their guard against deception of every sort, and rendering them those little favors which I myself, at the time above adverted to, stood so much in need of."

Before he had learned his way around his new ship, the recruit would be introduced to the daily routine. As soon as the crew was initially assembled, the First Lieutenant, or Executive Officer as he was later to be called, organized the men into two watches — starboard and larboard or port watches — and designated those who were to be forecastlemen, foretopmen, maintopmen, mizzentopmen, and afterguards. The "four on, eight off" of today's Navy or Merchant Marine would have seemed very soft indeed to a *Constellation* salt.

The duties of each group were well defined. The forecastlemen worked from the foremast forward, the foretopmen aloft and on the port side from the foremast to the mainmast, and the maintopmen aloft and on the starboard side from the foremast to the mainmast. The mizzentopmen carried out the work aloft and on the port side from the mainmast aft, while the afterguards were responsible for the starboard side aft. So well were these limits of a man's duties understood that a foretopman would look with contempt on a midshipman who directed him to "squilgee down" in the starboard gangway and would call one of the maintopmen to look after his own part of the ship. Competition was fierce.

Petty officers would be selected to fill the posts of: the master-at-arms, who served as the chief of police and had charge of the berthdeck, two ship's corporals or master-at-arms' mates, four coxswains, two captains of the forecastle, two captains of each of the tops (fore, main, and mizzen), two captains of the afterguard, two boatswain's mates, one gunner's mate, four quarter gunners, and so on down the list until all the rates had been filled. Privileges and extra pay came with petty officership; Strength, experience, and a clean record were the criteria for promotion.

The "station bill" would then be made out and each man required to learn his station for every evolution by noting his hammock number and referring to the bill which was nailed up in a prominent place for ready inspection. By this means he would learn the exact part of the ship to which he must go on the double when the order was given for "getting under weigh," "bringing ship to anchor," "tacking ship," "wearing ship," "loosing and furling," "reefing topsails," "in and out of boats," "up and down topgallant and royal yards," and many other tactics required in working a ship under sail.

Stations at "quarters" were similarly assigned so that each hand knew where he was to report when the ship was cleared for action. Eight or more men were assigned to each gun and the guns grouped in divisions, each of which was placed in the charge of a commissioned officer. A powder division, which was usually headed by the Second Lieutenant who was also the Navigator, was assigned the duty of passing the ammunition from the magazine to the gunners on the gun and spar decks.

At sea the men were exercised at "great guns" daily. Each gun crew had to train until it worked in unison, quickly, carefully, and with disdain for the flaming death that leaped towards them from beyond the slender wooden bulwarks and the thin hammock nettings that were the only protection against round shot, cannister, grape, and splinters.

If the recruit was a husky lad and looked as though he could pull a strong oar he might be assigned to one of the boat crews. In choosing men for this duty the First Lieutenant who wanted the best men available, was likely to be confronted by a complaint from one of the "captains" that too many men had been taken from his part of the ship and that he was left short-handed to carry out his work.

The twenty-four hours of the day were divided into five 4-hour watches — the names of which have varied with the years — and two 2-hour dogwatches that fell between 4 P.M. and 8 P.M. Sometime in the distant past the dogwatches had been established to make the number of watches eneven, so that the men would not have to stand the same watches day after day.

At dawn the Boatswain piped "Up all hammocks" which was answered by his mates' "Rise and shine." At the cry, "lash and stow," the hammocks were emptied, taken from their hooks, and lashed up in double time. None of the crew wanted to be the "last man out" as the Master's mates' ability to find unpleasant penalties such as scouring the galley smokestack with brick dust and rags was well known. Within a matter of minutes there was a rush for the ladders leading to the spar deck nettings where the hammocks were stowed for the day. Thus, the gun and berth decks were cleared.

"D'ye hear there, get your holystones and sand!" was the next command and the men collected around the forehatch where buckets, holystones, squilgees, and brooms were passed up from below. The holystones were so named because men worked the decks on their knees when holystoning. Water was drawn from over the side in buckets or a hose attached to handy billy pumps in the fore and main channels. The deck was then wet down and scoured with the holystones while the Boatswain's mates and midshipmen watched with keen eyes to see that no corner was missed. The work continued until the deck was spotless. The guns were cast loose and run in and out to enable some of the men to drag the heavy holystones back and forth over the deck where they had been secured, while others on hands and knees scoured the "hard to get at" places with smaller stones called "prayer books." The paint work was scrubbed with sand and canvas and the task finally completed with a second washing down of the deck and the stowing of the cleaning gear.

If the ship was at anchor, "a hand from each part of the

ship" was called away to board the catamarans alongside and
scrub the sides of the hull and copper sheathing above the
waterline with brooms, brushes, sand, and canvas. These men
were called side cleaners.

Seven bells (7:30 A.M.) was the signal for the men to wash
and clean up before hurrying on deck where the Master-at-
arms, rattan cane in hand, was waiting to hurry the laggards
along. "Come, toe the line!" was ordered and the sections fell
in for inspection. Each man was carefully scrutinized by the
Master-at-arms and his name was called out to the Officer-of-
the-Deck, who nodded his approval, as he passed muster.
When all had been passed, the formation was dismissed.

At five minutes before 8 A.M., the Officer-of-the-Deck reported 8 bells to the Captain, who might direct that the topgallant and royals be crossed or the sails set, if the ship was
in port. If the yards were to be crossed, all hands were called,
the yards sent up, and at the third roll of the drum, the yards
were swung across, the ensign raised to the peak, the commission pennant changed from the short pennant flown at
night to the forty foot long "whip," and the bell struck eight
times. The band played and the day officially began. The men
could have had two to three hours of work before this moment.

The mess cooks appeared from the galley, their arms laden
with pots of tea and scouse, and breakfast was piped. At noon
"Up spirits" was piped, and the daily issue of grog — half
whiskey and at least half water — was made. As each man
received his "tot," he carried it to the space on deck, hatch or
mess chest allotted his mess, laid the red tarpaulin mess
cloth, and on it spread the mess gear of wooden or pewter
plates and bone-handled cutlery for the first meal of the day.

The week's menu was fixed by the same Act of Congress in
1794, that authorized the construction of the *Constellation*
and was varied only on special occasions. This table of
allowances provided for the substitution of one quart of beer
for one half pint of spirits, but did not specify whether the
choice was made by the seaman or the purser. The
meat—salted beef or pork—was usually preserved, although
fresh was provided when possible. Salt beef was called "salt

horse." The bread, commonly called "hard tack," was hard biscuit which was baked ashore. The peas, beans, and rice were dried. Vegetables and fruit were issued when available. All food was either stewed or boiled, and was not cooked well, with only a single galley stove for the use of the entire crew. Though sometimes in a spoiled condition after weeks at sea in tropical waters, the rations, nevertheless, were hearty. American vessels, unlike their British or French counterparts, were known as "feeders."

SUNDAY	1½ pounds beef, 1 pound bread, ½ pint rice, ½ pint spirits
MONDAY	1 pound pork, 1 pound bread, ½ pint peas, 4 ounces cheese, ½ pint spirits
TUESDAY	1½ pounds beef, 1 pound bread, 1 pound potatoes, ½ pint spirits
WEDNESDAY	1 pound pork, 1 pound bread, 2 ounces butter, ½ pint spirits or in lieu - ½ pint rice, 4 ounces cheese, 6 ounces molasses
THURSDAY	1 pound pork, 1 pound bread, ½ pint peas, ½ pint spirits
FRIDAY	1 pound bread, 1 pound potatoes, 1 pound salt fish, 2 ounces butter or 1 gill of oil, ½ pint spirits
SATURDAY	1 pound pork, 1 pound bread, ½ pint peas, 4 ounces cheese, ½ pint spirits

While breakfast was being eaten, the Boatswain's pipe might again sound the call for attention and the uniform of the day announced. If it was other than the workday clothes usually worn, sea bags were broken out, the proper clothing chosen and donned, and the bags retied and restowed in their proper places. While officers and warrant officers wore uniforms as specified by the Navy Department, the men dressed pretty much as they pleased until 1817. Most the them either acquired clothing—which they had to buy—from the purser, who bought in quantity, or made their own clothes out of available canvas. After the ship had been at sea for a short time, a degree of uniformity was attained.

In the meantime, the Surgeon's mate made his morning visit to the sick bay to examine and treat those on the binnacle list and to check up on the attentiveness of the loblolly boys. One of the boys was assigned the duty of making the rounds of the decks, ringing a bell to announce sick call; the dressing board was brought up, and the invalids collected on the half deck for the Surgeon's attention.

A full hour was usually allotted for each meal and as soon as breakfast was finished and the mess clothes rolled up and stowed in the niches between the deck beams and ledges, a crowd collected around the galley. Smoking was permitted, and the latest newspapers, politics, the ship's movements, and the current scuttlebutt were discussed.

When 2 bells (9 A.M.) in the forenoon watch were struck, the Boatswain's pipe announced the end of the breakfast hour and the Master's mate shouted the order "All hands on deck!" At this signal the sweepers turned to and each man cleaned the area which was his responsibility. At the sound of the drum beat to quarters, each man hurried to take his battle station for the Lieutenant's inspection. This might be followed by an exercise at the guns, boats, yards and sails, manual of arms, or broadsword drill. Small arms and cutlasses were stowed in the armory and broken out when needed, under the supervision of the Master-at-arms.

After quarters, the real work of the day began: the carpenter, the sailmaker, the cooper and their mates, working on the larboard side of the gun deck, resumed the jobs "secured" when the previous day's work ended. The marines busied themselves with drills and putting their accoutrements in order, and the midshipmen and apprentice boys retired to the screened off areas on the starboard side of the gun deck where their instructors endeavored to teach them the rudiments of their professions. Abreast the forehatch, the boatswain's and sailmaker's mates busied themselves with needle, palm, and fid, repairing fenders, oars, pumps, boots and shoes, while the tailors, with cabbage, shears and thread, carried on their trade in another part of the deck.

On Thursday mornings the men scrubbed their hammocks, and on Fridays, they were given the opportunity to wash their own clothes. Water was drawn from over the side, buckets of sand brought from ballast below, and those who were lucky enough to possess a bit of soap took care that it did not disappear when their backs were turned. Brushes made with coir, the prepared fiber of the husks of coconuts, were highly valued and in great demand as they scrubbed the canvas clean with a minimum of effort, but their use was forbidden on many ships because of the havoc they wrought on the fabrics to which they were applied. In practice they were widely used, forbidden or not.

After the 9 o'clock inspection on Wednesdays and Saturdays, one of the mess cooks, who had been designated the official ship's barber, set up his chair on the gun deck and announced himself ready to serve those of the crew who needed a shave or a haircut. Whether the quality of his work left something to be desired or whether it was the fashion of the day, some of the crew grew beards and left their locks untrimmed.

Meanwhile, the cooks on the berth deck were busy arranging their mess chests for the Master-at-arm's inspection, when every pot and pan must "in fancy row upon the chest-lid of the bag-rack show." Every spit box had to be in line with its staves scraped clean and its hoops polished, and woe betide the one whose kits were not spotless!

And so the forenoon hours were passed. At 7 bells (11:30 A.M.) all work ceased, sweepers were again piped, and a "clean sweep down fore and aft" ordered. When the sun had reached its meridian, the Officer-of-the-Deck reported to the Captain that noon had arrived and was told to "Make it so." Eight bells were struck and the Boatswain and his mates piped the call for grog and dinner.

By 1 bell (12:30 P.M.) in the afternoon watch, dinner was over and the smokers had repaired to the galley to resume the debates started at breakfast. At 2 bells, the Boatswain again piped "All hands" — some to work and some to have the next two hours for their own pursuits. Those who were standing the watch below devoted their time to overhauling their sea bags, reading, working on hobbies or fancy rope work, ship models, or scrimshaw, or caulking off between the guns. The apprentice boys, released from their morning's classroom work, took the occasion to blow off steam by sky-larking on the forecastle. The less serious-minded oldsters whose presence was not required on deck, disappeared below, certain of finding a dice game in some out-of-the-way corner considered safe from the prying eyes of the Master-at-arms and his mates.

At 8 bells (4 P.M.), the Boatswain piped the order to "Clear the decks!" At this order the industrious members of the crew "secured" for the day, the gamblers halted their play, **the apprentice boys stopped their gambols, and the day's work** came to an end. During a wartime cruise, however, most afternoons were spent at the guns, and in a chase men might stand twelve to fourteen hours at the ready or in action.

Supper was piped and quickly finished during the first dogwatch. In good weather the entire crew, from the old salt nearing seventy winters to the apprentice boy of twelve, gathered on the spar deck where they could watch the setting sun and enjoy the evening breeze. In the larboard gangway near the formast's fife rail, a group gathered to hear a bearded veteran spin a yarn; farther forward a checker game was in progress. Aft of the foremast, a group was heatedly discussing the latest intelligence from the last newspaper that had been brought aboard. The end of the second dogwatch was signaled by the Boatswain's piping "Stand by your hammocks," and the crowd dispersed, each man to take up his position in line abreast the hammock netting in which his hammock has been stowed for the day.

At the commands "Lay up," and "Uncover!" the men detailed as hammock stowers swung themselves up on the nettings and threw back the cloths; "Pipe down!" was followed by the cries of the stowers calling out the number of each hammock removed, the odd numbers belonging to the starboard watch and the even numbers to the port watch. As his number was called each man stepped forward to catch his hammock, carry it below and sling it in its appointed place. The oldsters soon retired to escape the din that was likely to ensue when the younger tars collected between the guns and, with accordion, banjo, song, and tall tales passed the time until tattoo.

Just before 8 bells (8 P.M.), the First Lieutenant made his evening rounds of the ship, reported everything secure to the

Captain, and the first watch was set as the bell struck the hour. The sunset gun was fired, the colors hauled down, and the short commission pennant broken out as the long "whip" came down.

At 8:45, the fifes and drums struck up one of the popular tunes of the day and the concert was continued until 9 o'clock when tattoo was sounded and the Officer-of-the-Deck gave the order "Roll off!" At the third roll of the drum the bell struck the hour, the Boatswain's pipes shrilled "Pipe down!" and all those not on watch turned in. The seamen who had remained on deck sought a soft plank on which they could stretch out, and only the lookouts, the men at the wheel, and the sentries walking their posts remained alert. Silence enveloped the ship—a silence broken only by the soft slapping of water along the sides, the creak of the lines and blocks in the rigging, and the half-hourly reports of the lookouts to the Officer-of-the-Deck.

Sunday's routine differed from weekdays in that only the necessary work of operating the ship was carried out. After a special cleaning from the spar to the lower decks, the crew donned its best uniforms and repaired to the area about the mainmast where church services were conducted. After the services were over the Captain stepped forward, read the Articles of War, and each man walked around the capstan to undergo the Captain's critical scrutiny of his cleanliness and general bearing. This ordeal having been completed, the formation was dismissed and the men were free to lounge about the deck until the issuing of the pre-dinner grog ration was announced and the noon meal piped. On Sunday afternoon, the members of the ship's company— with the exception of those required to work the ship—were free to do as they pleased. Those who could read often broke out their Bibles, and it was not unusual for an older sailor to teach a ship's boy to read with the Bible as his only textbook.

In those days before travelling U.S.O. shows, movies, and organized recreation on board ships, sailors were left to their own resources to find diversions with which to combat the inevitable boredom of a long cruise. Some crews took up a collection after getting under way, and, at the first port of call, purchased the supplies necessary to stage theatricals. Aspiring thespians were never lacking, and after sufficient time had elapsed to sew the costumes, prepare the stage settings, and rehearse the players, the production would be presented from a stage set up by enclosing the quarterdeck from the mainmast with sails. The officers, their chairs carried out from their mess, would enjoy the performances from a vantage point but never participated in them. A ship's library was usually maintained in the fore-passage and the collection of the works of the popular authors and poets of the day enjoyed a wide circulation.

The Boatswain's announcement that an auction was to be held marked another red-letter day, and when the Purser's steward came on deck bearing an assortment of abandoned or lost bags and hammocks that were to be sold, all other diversions were forgotten. The appearance of the Master-at-arms, who acted as auctioneer, was the signal for a crowd to collect; and when silence had been obtained the contents of the bags were displayed and knocked down to the highest bidder. The fact that the article of clothing that he had bought proved to be too large or too small for his personal use or that it was beyond repair, did not lessen the sailor's enjoyment of his purchase: It could always be traded off to a shipmate for some other coveted article.

The lot of a commissioned officer in a frigate was only a shade better than that of the enlisted men. The same elements of crowding, monotony, and lack of privacy were to be found in the wardroom as well as in the forward part of the ship.

The average roster of officers in the *Constellation* numbered six or seven commissioned officers who lived, messed, and entertained their guests in a compartment less than twenty feet wide by thirty feet long. On reporting aboard, each officer was assessed a predetermined sum for the purchase of crockery, table linen, and flatware for the wardroom mess and his mess bill for the ensuing month was collected. If the mess decided to lay in a supply of wine and spirits, an additional sum was assessed.

A caterer, traditionally the purser but later the paymaster, was elected and put in charge of the menus and business affairs of the mess. According to naval regulations, each officer received one ration of food worth twenty-five cents and one ration of spirits worth five cents.

A "lunch" was served at 8 A.M., a "regular meat breakfast" at 11 A.M., and a course dinner that was followed by wines and cigars at 5 P.M. Seating at the wardroom table was strictly according to protocol with the First Lieutenant at the head and forward end of the table, and the caterer at the foot. The ship's lieutenants and master were ranged according to rank on the starboard side while the other commissioned officers, surgeon, chaplain, marine captain and lieutenants occupied the port side of the table. A midshipman was usually invited to share the evening meal with his superiors. Even the Captain, who had a private mess, might occasionally condescend to accept an invitation to dine with his officers.

Four officers were usually on deck during each watch. The senior lieutenant acted as Officer-of-the-Deck and was in charge of the operation of the ship during the four hours that he had the "duty." The newly fledged midshipman soon learned that the weather side of the quarterdeck at sea, and the starboard side at anchor were to be kept clear for the exclusive use of the Captain and the Officer-of-the-Deck, and that the latter always relinquished it when the former appeared.

When their presence was not required on deck, the officers spent most of their off-duty hours in the wardroom, or trying to sleep or study in the box-like staterooms. Games of checkers, chess, or backgammon were usually in progress, and few cruises were completed without a budding musician turning up to torture the ears of the other men in the room until the Master-at-arms' discreet knock on the door at 10 P.M. to announce that "lights and fires on board are extinguished."

Thus, a day on the Yankee Racehorse came to close.

Every Inch a Sailor

The first cruise of the *Constellation* produced no prizes, but was invaluable in giving Truxtun an opportunity to get his officers and men organized into a fighting unit to test the qualities of his ship. The cruise down the Bay from Patuxent to Hampton Roads had been prolonged by long calms and adverse winds, but in his letter of June 23, 1798, to the Secretary of War he remarked that "the Frigate goes through the water with great Swiftness indeed" and that he was looking forward to having "Opportunities to try her Sailing by and large."

Once Cape Henry was astern, *Constellation* had ample opportunity to test her mettle as she stood to the eastward. After leaving her convoy some twenty leagues east of the Cape, she turned southward and encountered varying winds that rose to gale strength, rain, and thunderstorms. An occasional interval of good weather allowed the crew to dry their soaked clothing and hammocks on the spar deck. The Purser reported that some of the bread had been damaged and 28¾ bushels of potatoes found to be rotten were duly surveyed by a board consisting of the First Lieutenant, Master, Carpenter, and Boatswain and dumped over the side. Truxtun's report to the Secretary of War that he was able to deliver to a pilot boat while cruising off Charleston on July 16, stated that "I have a clean, healthy Ship, and have no Doubt, but in case of Need, my Men will freely do their Duty. I have endeavored to attach them to the naval Service, by mild Treatment, and rigid Justice . . . The Ship behaves well in all Sorts of Weather, and sails fast, but from being caulked in the Winter, her upper Works are open."

On July 21, Truxtun reached the southern limit of his patrol and reversed course. Bad weather continued to plague him and living conditions aboard the frigate were uncomfortable. On July 23, *Constellation* logged her first death, Ordinary Seaman Patrick Leonard who had "an old sore Leg, and a Complication of Disorders . . . his Body was committed to the Deep, with the usual Ceremonies." Next day Truxtun ordered "six Fires at least to be made in Pots on the Birth Deck to purify the Air, and dry the Apartments of the People." He also ordered that at least "six large Fires (be made) below, under the care of the Carpenter, and his Crew" on Monday, Thursday, and Saturday of each week, and that on alternate days the crew's quarters were to be washed with vinegar or fumigated with "Devil's" (brimstone), the standard "cure" for scurvy. Truxtun was a more considerate skipper than most. Few commanders would allow fires below, even though the heat was needed to warm and dry the men.

July 28 found *Constellation* off Charleston again, and a pilot boat came alongside to deliver mail and take Truxtun's reports ashore. He was waited on by a delegation of Charleston merchants who requested him to go to Havana to convoy a number of their merchantmen home; but Truxtun had no authority to deviate from the patrol area to which he had been assigned and referred them to the government.

Throughout the cruise Truxtun endeavored to keep his officers and men on their toes to improve the efficiency of the ship. General quarters were sounded whenever a "chace" was in progress and constant drill and "exercises" were held. On July 12, Midshipman William Davis was appointed Acting Lieutenant at Arms—approximately the equivalent of a modern gunnery officer—and on July 30, Truxtun's longstanding dissatisfaction with his Lieutenant of Marines came to a head.

TO LIEUTENANT TRIPLETT OF MARINES.

Sir, Had I exercised my Authority as the Commander of this Ship, and arrested in all Cases, where many in my Situation would not have hesitated a Moment. The *Constellation* must 'ere now, have exhibited for the Out set of a Navy, a sad Spectacle indeed, to the People of the United States. But, Sir, I have cast a Veil, or Curtain over so many Improprieties, and Neglects, from Tenderness, and Delicacy to Gentlemen's Characters, and in Hopes daily of more Attention, and Regularity; the Patience, and temper in me is now nearly exhausted.—As I know full well, that it is much easier to make a deep Wound, than to heal a small one, I have been actuated in my Conduct to you by Principles mild and inherent in my Nature, believing at the same Time, that a little Reflection would induce you to appreciate the Measures I have taken, to make your Duty plain, and easy, and excite you to a more minute Attention thereto . . . I have hitherto been disappointed, I can no longer continue disobeyed, If I am, Recourse must be had to an Alternative, by no Means pleasant to me, or honorable to you . . . I hope, therefore, the present will have the desired effect, and in that Hope, I remain

Your most Obedt humble Servt

THOMAS TRUXTUN

N.B. Two Vessels were brought to, and spoke last Night, when you was not on deck.—Under the Orders I gave you, it was as much your Duty, to leave Directions for the Sergeant of the Watch, to call you, as I consider it mine to be called on certain Occasions, by the Officer of the Watch, and not wait for all Hands to be called, when I deem it unnecessary, in speaking trifling Merchantmen.

Petty officers who got out of line were similarly treated, and when it was found that Daniel Gorman, the Master's Mate, was guilty of pilfering the rum casks in the hold, Truxtun "accordingly suspended him from ever again acting in that Capacity under my Authority in this, or any other Public Ship whatever, that I may command."

On July 7, Congress had passed "An Act declaring the treaties heretofore concluded with France, no longer obligatory on the United States," and the cruising range of American warships was extended beyond the territorial waters of the country. Three days after the act had been signed, Secretary Stoddert suggested that, with the exception of one frigate, one sloop-of-war, and the revenue cutters which were to be kept at home for coastal defense, all the United States' men-of-war should be sent to the West Indies "to keep up incessant attacks upon French cruisers on their own ground." Stoddert's suggestion was approved by President Adams.

On August 10, *Constellation* was ordered to proceed to Havana "without delay" in company with the 20-gun sloop *Baltimore,* for the purpose of convoying back home some sixty American merchantmen, loaded with cargoes worth over a million dollars. Finding his small stores almost depleted, Truxtun put into Hampton Roads for supplies, and made such repairs as necessary before the autumnal equinox brought more foul weather.

Word of *Constellation's* mission to Havana was "leaked" in Baltimore, and Truxtun was embarrassed when merchantmen from that port, Alexandria, and Delaware began to assemble in the roads and inform him that they had been ordered to join a convoy to Havana. Truxtun, who had had no word from the Secretary of the Navy that he was to take an outward bound convoy under his wing, dispatched an open letter to the Navy Agent in Baltimore: "I am therefore not a little afraid, that something is wrong . . . We have no Doubt, many bad People in this extensive Country, and if the Destination of Ships are known Weeks before their Departure; pilot Boats may be dispatched with Information to the Enemy, who will no doubt benefit thereby."

Unwilling to deviate from his orders,Truxtun wrote to the Secretary of the Navy for instructions; but, without waiting for a reply he agreed next day to convoy the ships whose speed was sufficient to keep up with the *Constellation* and the *Baltimore.* A detailed code of signals for use between the escort and convoy was distributed, a new Lieutenant of Marines shipped, and final preparation made for sea. The signal for getting underway was made at 6 A.M. on September 1. Before the maneuver could be executed, however, the wind hauled around from north northwest to northeast and, combined with a strong flood tide, compelled Truxtun to haul down his signal for weighing and "put to Service on the Cable."

Strong easterly winds continued for three days. On the morning of September 4, they shifted to the west and the convoy got underway at dawn, but by noon the winds were so light that anchors were let go within a league of the Cape Henry Lighthouse. The convoy waited until the tidal current had turned and the wind had veered to the south. At 4 P.M., it once again got underway and by evening was heading toward Cuba.

Constellation's log on the outward bound voyage records variable weather, routine shipboard activities, and the loss of Seaman John Cole, who fell overboard. Unidentified vessels were brought to and examined, news exchanged, and inquiries made about the presence of French ships in the area. None had been sighted. Two Marines were put in the brig for sleeping on duty, but Captain Truxtun chose to take a lenient view of the offense and wrote Lieutenant Saunders:

> It is at all Times very unpleasant to flog Men, if it can in any Way be avoided, and in an infant, and totally unorganized Navy, Ways and Means more mild, should be devised to correct Inattention, Neglect, and other Faults . . . I have duly considered the Complaint made against the two Marines under Confinement, and of every Circumstance, that can in any Way tend to promote the Good of the American Navy; but our peculiar Situation must be taken into View, and altho' the Crime of sleeping upon Duty, is a very heinous one, we will once more pardon the Offence, and release from Confinement the two Men in Question, on their Promise of not doing the like again; but at the same Time they will receive a Reprimand from you & be informed that half the Allowance of Rum is to be stopped, untill the first Day of October next ensuing. (3 weeks)

At 11 A.M. September 21, the convoy sailed past Morro Castle and into the harbor while *Constellation* stood off the entrance of the harbor with *Baltimore* in company. Truxtun had hoped to make a quick turn-around at Havana and return with the merchantmen then in port, but, on the request of the U.S. Consul, agreed to postpone his departure until additional ships in the vicinity could join. A convoy of forty-three vessels was finally assembled and left Havana on the evening of September 29, with strict orders from Truxtun that they sail in close order.

In spite of the orders and signals given each master before sailing, the merchantmen paid little attention to the convoy commodore. In his journal entry of October 6, a week after sailing from Havana, Truxtun voiced frustration: "Twenty seven Sail of the Convoy in Sight, many of which pay but little Attention to Signals or to our Lights at Night."

Belvidere and *America* of Philadelphia, which were armed

and swift sailers, left the convoy within a few days in company with several other fast ships, but not, Truxtun observed, until they were clear of all danger from French privateers.

Foul weather harassed the convoy from the start and Truxtun noted that "we have had a succession of Easterly and Northerly Winds, Gale after Gale, in Fact, we have not had one Hour of fair Wind, since leaving our Station off Morro Castle." On October 3, *Harmony* of Charleston, South Carolina, collided with *Dolphin* of Boston, and both *Constellation* and *Baltimore* answered her signal of distress. On October 6, the brig *Fair Eliza* of Bristol, Rhode Island, sprung a leak and *Constellation's* carpenter was sent aboard to repair the damage.

On October 9, they were abeam of the *Typee* heading to Savannah, Georgia, and Truxtun felt that any danger from French privateers was past. The convoy was signaled to break up and the merchantmen were told that they were on their own. *Baltimore* was detached and ordered to patrol up the coast to Charleston and, after laying off and on that port for four days, to rendezvous with *Constellation* in Hampton Roads.

On October 21, it was discovered that *Constellation's* rudder head had split and the spare tiller was shipped in the cabin. *Constellation* continued on her northerly course, a few of the convoy keeping within sight of her in spite of the foul weather and head seas. At 10 A.M. October 24, Cape Henry Light was sighted and *Constellation* came to anchor in its lee on the following day.

The dispatches brought aboard by the Norfolk pilot boat included one of October 13, from the Secretary of the Navy ordering *Constellation* to continue her patrol until November tenth. She should then proceed to New York if Truxtun thought she could cross the bar safely, otherwise go on to Newport. On arrival at either port, she was to take on provisions and other stores for a six months' cruise. Truxtun acknowledged the orders, but stated that because of narrow design none of the new frigates could stow six months' stores. Lieutenant Cowper was detached to go to Norfolk to recruit sixteen seamen to fill *Constellation's* complement, and the crew was put to work cleaning up the ship and repairing the rudder.

Secretary Stoddert's order to prepare for a six months' cruise suggested to Truxtun that *Constellation* would be sent to the Caribbean. A survey of her sea worthiness revealed that the storms she encountered had wreaked havoc with her rigging, and that her sails were thin due to "bad Canvass." The ring of one of her remaining anchors was also not to be trusted. Under the circumstances, Truxtun demurred at taking his ship north at that time of year. In his letter to the Secretary of the Navy he also pointed out that *Constellation* had never received any of the grape shot originally requisitioned, nor had he been able to get a replacement for the bower anchor lost in June. As the frigate could only carry provisions for three to four months, Truxtun suggested that if they were going to the Caribbean, the Navy Department might consider sending a store ship to Martinique, where the U.S. warships could call for supplies.

Truxtun's guess that *Constellation* would be sent to the Caribbean for the winter was confirmed by orders dated December 8:

It is the desire of the President, that our navy Should be employed in the West Indies, this Winter, in protecting our commerce and punishing the depredations on it, from the French Islands—

Your Frigate being ready for Sea, it will proceed with all dispatch; and by such course as you shall judge most likely to fall in with French Cruisers; to the Island of St. Christophers, taking under your Command, the Brigantine *Richmond* Capt. Barron, and the Virginia Cutter Capt. Bright, and if the Ship *Baltimore* Capt Phillips, should have returned to Norfolk, take her also, and if otherwise leave orders for Phillips to proceed after you, to join you in the West Indies, as soon as he can take in the necessary provisions at Norfolk. When the Schooner *Retaliation* of 14 Guns & the Brig *Norfolk* of 18 Guns return from their present service, either one or both of these Vessels, will be added to your force.—You will direct your operations from St. Christophers, as far Leeward as Porto Rico, paying attention to St. Martins and that Group of Islands, called the Virgin Gorda; and wherever else between St. Christophers and Porto Rico, your judgement shall direct you. --- Capt Barry, with two Frigates under his command, and several Ships of considerable force, will rendezvous at Prince Ruperts bay, in the Island of Dominica, and will attend to every thing to the windward of St. Christophers; but it is not meant to confine you Strictly to the Cruising Grounds, thus pointed out for you; but that you should depart therefrom occasionally, as Circumstances in your Judgement shall require.—. . . Should you be incumbered with French prisoners, your first Effort must be to exchange them for our own Citizens, in the Hands of the French. You can not take too much pains to effect this desirable object. It will be better to give more than Man for Man, than suffer our meritorious Seaman to remain in their hands, and no Bargain will be thought a bad one which shall relieve them from Captivity.. . . You have heretofore received your Authority founded upon the existing Laws to capture French armed Vessels wherever found on the high Sea, and to recapture our own Vessels taken by them.—You will however, have it understood by those under your Command, that being at peace with all the rest of the World, and wishing to remain so, the Vessels and people of other Nations, must experience from us civility, and Friendship; Our Laws will not even permit the Recapture of our Vessels, taken by the Vessels, of any of the Nations at War, except the French, and it must be presumed, that the Courts of such Nations will render Justice, where such captures are illegal.—The President commands me to express to you, his high Confidence in your Ability, Bravery, Enterprise, and Zeal, for your Country's Interest & honor; and his full Assurance, that the honor of the American Flag, will never be tarnished in your hands.—And he desires me to add as a particular request, that you will excite as much as possible in the Officers under your Command, such a Spirit as ought to animate, such Men engaged in such a Cause; and a high respect for the Honor of our Flag.

The final weeks of December were occupied with making the last preparations for sea and attending to the details of the frigate's administration. Lieutenant of Marines Bartholomew Clinch was welcomed aboard to replace Lieutenant Triplett and was given written as of his specific duties. He also received copies of Truxtun's orders to Triplett.

On December 16, Truxtun submitted the name of John Rodgers for promotion to captain, but was advised by the Secretary of the Navy that the nomination could not be submitted to the Senate before the *Constellation* was due to sail. He thought it advisable to wait awhile and submit Rodger's name with one or two other lieutenants to avoid jealousy and a charge of favoritism.

The last day of the year 1798 found *Constellation* in comp'.ny with the 18-gun brig *Richmond,* under Captain Samuel Barrow. They rounded Cape Henry, bound for the Caribbean with a convoy of four merchantmen and the schooner *Thetis.* The weather was ideal for the first week but *Thetis* was a dull sailer and her master paid but little attention to Truxtun's signals. Progress was slow and Truxtun had to regulate his canvas to keep her in sight.

On January 11, Truxtun's journal noted that he had discoverd—by lunar observations for longitude a lost art in navigation—that a very strong current was setting them to westward. They were also fifty leagues to leeward of the course they were steering by dead reckoning.

By January 12, the convoy was between Barbadoes and Nevis. *Richmond* was then detached to convoy the schooners *Little John* and *President* to St. Thomas, while *Constellation* proceeded to Martinique with *Thetis* under her wing. On the following day, they spoke an English schooner from which reported that the frigate *United States* was in the harbor, several United States men-of-war were in Dominica, and that two French men-of-war were anchored at Guadeloupe.

They were within four leagues of St. Pierre on January 14, and saw no evidence of French cruisers in the vicinity, *Thetis* was ordered to proceed to her anchorage in the harbor, while *Constellation* then steered for St. Christopher's. On the following day *Constellation* met the 44-gun British frigate *Concorde*. She learned that there was only one French frigate, 44-gun *Le Volantaire,* and a corvette at Baseterre, Guadeloupe; and, that *L'Insurgente* and *La Pence* had sailed from that port on January 1, to carry the infamous Victor Hughes, "the Robespierre of the West Indies," back to France as a prisoner.

During the afternoon of January 16, *Constellation* sighted Captain Barry's squadron which consisted of the 44-gun frigate *United States,* the 20-gun sloop-of-war *Montezuma,* under Captain Murray, and the 18-gun sloop of war *Norfolk,* under Captain Williams, with a convoy of twenty five merchantmen northbound from Prince Ruperts Bay, Dominica. Captain Barry in *United States* held his course, but the others hove to and Captain Murray came aboard. As Barry had refused to accompany the convoy, Truxtun was asked to take charge and agreed to sail with them until they reached St. Christopher's (St. Kitts). Murray was shown the orders that *Norfolk* was to join Truxtun's squadron after he had escorted the convoy to Latitude 25° North. *Norfolk* was then ordered to make a quick run up to Antigua, to round up any vessels there that might want to join the convoy, and to rendezvous with the main group at St. Kitts.

At 2 P.M., the convoy was abeam Montserrat, and Truxtun signaled *Montezuma* to take the lead into the anchorage at Basseterre while he protected the rear. Lieutenant of Marines Clinch was sent ashore with a message to the commanding officer of the fort identifying the fleet and arranging for salutes. At 5 P.M., *Constellation* dropped her anchor in the Basseterre Roads and exchanged a thirteen-gun salute with the fort. Within the hour a boat came alongside bearing Captain Matson of His Britannic Majesty's ship *Cyane*—which was later to run afoul of the U.S. Navy in the War of 1812—Sir Patrick Blake, and a delegation of citizens of the island. Courtesies were exchanged, and on the following day Truxtun went ashore to make his official call on the Governor and return the calls he had received. In his report to the Secretary of the Navy Truxtun gave the details of the cruise, spoke of the cordial reception received at St. Kitts, and advised the Secretary that he had contacted a merchant there, who would accept and disburse supplies sent to the squadron from home.

The convoy departed on January 21, with *Montezuma* and *Norfolk* as escorts. As *Richmond* had returned from St. Thomas, Captain Barron was dispatched to Antigua to bring down any merchantmen there and at Montserrat, while *Constellation* collected others from St. Bartholomew, Nevis, and the islands to leeward as far as St. Thomas. As the squadron now had a base of sorts, Truxtun sent his spare topmasts and spars ashore with the launch, to make "the Ship more clear, and in better Condition for carrying Sail."

Constellation got underway during the morning of January 22, and shaped a course running between St. Kitts and the island of St. Eustatius. Her purpose was to cruise off St. Martins and St. Bartholomew so that Truxtun could gather more information on the whereabouts of the French cruisers. Two days later, while cruising off Gustavia on St. Bartholomew, a schooner and a ship were sighted; the ship immediately made for the port, but the schooner was brought to and boarded. She proved to be of Swedish registry, bound for Guadeloupe her master told Truxtun that the ship was an armed French vessel.

Constellation stood on and off the port through a night of foul weather. When two American brigs came out in the morning, Truxtun agreed to convoy them until they were clear of St. Martins and other French-held islands. On January 27, he was off of Montserrat looking for American vessels that wished a convoy home. He then steered for Guadeloupe. At 5 P.M., he chased a small sloop under the "Land of Bassateere" but when he lost her in a squall, wore around and headed for St. Kitts. There, he expected to rendezvous with *Richmond* and the merchantmen that had been collected for convoy.

The convoy and *Richmond* were awaiting his arrival and were immediately ordered to make sail with the sloop-of-war to escort them as far as Latitude 20° North. *Constellation* then turned back for Guadeloupe, and by noon of the 29th was on her station off Basseterre, Guadeloupe, where the 44-gun frigate *Le Volontaire*, and the French corvette were within sight in the harbor.

On January 30, *Constellation* hoisted her colors hoping that the French ships would come out. When they showed no interest in his challenge, Truxtun sailed north along the coast where French privateers with their prizes were known to lurk while awaiting an opportunity to get into Basseterre.

The patrol was uneventful until February 1, when a sail was sighted and chased into the harbor of Fort St. Pine, Guadeloupe. Spoiling for a fight, Truxtun hoisted his colors and stood in toward the mouth of the bay until he was just out of range of the guns of the fort. Although he made several passes across the mouth of the harbor, the frigate refused to accept his challenge and come out. Circling the island, Truxtun taunted the forts as they passed, and stood off and on the French stronghold for a full week hoping that he could catch one of their ships beyond the protection of the guns on shore. Truxtun's journal notes that in the three-hour chase he gained three leagues on one Frenchman, and ruefully observes that "if we had been fortunate enough to have had her in a Direction to be chaced off the Land, instead of on it in one Hour more she would have been a Prize to the *Constellation.*" To add insult to injury, the French fort at the entrance to the harbor opened fire on *Constellation,* which was flying her ensign at the masthead. Truxtun replied to this with double the number of guns before coming about to chase seven sail that had appeared to the South Southwest. These proved to be three armed British ships bound for Liverpool with four American merchantmen under convoy.

Lady Luck was not yet ready to smile on the doughty captain and, as it was time to check with his squadron, Truxtun sailed *Constellation* for St. Kitts, where she came to anchor on February 3, 1799.

Into Battle

Two days at Basseterre were sufficient for Truxtun to get the reports of his captains and write their new orders, and make arrangements for the next northbound convoy to get under way on February 10. *Constellation* and *Norfolk* sailed on February 5 with the understanding that Captain Williams was to cruise to leeward until the convoy was to leave, while Truxtun patrolled to windward. The weather turned foul on the second day and continued squally and unpleasant with *Constellation* bucking head seas as Truxtun bore away to pass between the islands of Nevis and Redonda.

Just before noon on Feburary 9, the masthead lookout reported the sail of a large ship on the southern horizon. Captain Truxtun was in his cabin writing in his journal when the messenger brought the word from the Officer-of-the-Deck. He lost no time in reaching the quarterdeck. Seizing a glass, he leveled it in the direction and, sure enough, there she was: a big three-masted vessel with all sails set.

The order was immediately given to change course to intercept the stranger, but the boatswain's mates were told to let the men finish their noon meal. By one o'clock, the two ships were close enough to read each other's flag signals, and Truxtun hoisted the recognition signal for a British man-of-war—a blue flag at the fore topmast and a red, white, and blue flag on the mainmast. As he watched through his glass the stranger hoisted the Stars and Stripes. This incorrect reply aroused his suspicions, but to make sure, *Constellation's* captain ordered the recognition signal for an American man-of-war broken out. When the stranger made no reply, Truxtun ordered his men to quarters.

If you have ever seen or been a part of the swift but orderly rush of a modern man-of-war's men, responding to the spine-chilling clang of General Quarters Alarm and the harsh command over the 1 M.C. for "General Quarters, General Quarters! All hands man your battle stations!" then you have an idea of the port and starboard, forward and aft, aloft and below, flow of men and material answering the call to quarters aboard a wooden sailing warship. Merchant sailors have always derided the "impossibly" large number of men on a warship, not realizing that a man-of-war's crew must fight, sail, and repair damage all at the same time. In sailing days the ship's crew might also have to provide prize crews. Lastly, the crew was a body of infantry ready at all times to defend a floating fort or charge the enemy.

Gun ports yawed open and *Constellation* showed her row of teeth. Slow matches were lighted. Groups of sailors, under the command of junior officers, mustered at the pinrails, one group for each mast. Now, readying for battle, they had to sail the ship even better than ever. The magazine and shot locker were opened and boys formed the human passing chain. Below, under the command of the ship's carpenter and his mates, the damage control party waited, surveying the pumps, the wooden plugs, the oakum, the shoring beams, and the water buckets for fire—knowing that a white-hot round might at any moment come crashing and splintering through the bulkhead, or that a sudden combination of collision and flame would cause them to be trapped below decks.

In the cockpit the surgeon and his mates, along with the ship's purser and other non-combatants, prepared their saws and knives, ready for amputations; first-aid (even later medical treatment) was little more than cutting and bandaging. The quartermasters double-manned the wheel. Marines, having drawn their muskets, cutlasses, and side arms from the arms chest, moved aloft to man the fighting tops. Their job was to pick off the enemy officers and gunners on the weather deck.

Truxtun, his hands clasped behind his back, stood apart on the quarterdeck. Men and ship strained for his commands.

As the chase continued the stranger hauled her wind and stood to the northwestward. With *Constellation* gaining, it was evident that she would have to fight. The Stars and Stripes were hauled down, the French tricolor hoisted in its place, and a shot fired to windward to indicate that she was now showing her true colors. The Americans did not know it yet, but she was the 40-gun *L'Insurgente*, fastest frigate in the French Navy, and until recently under the command of the former American naval officer Joshua Barney. She was now skippered by Captain Citizen Barreaut.

When a sudden tropical squall struck both vessels at 2 P.M., she turned hoping to run for the neutral harbor of St. Eustatius, some thirty miles to the east, but *Constellation* continued to close on her while keeping to windward. Thanks to the discipline which Captain Truxtun had been drilling into his crew, *Constellation* weathered the gust without much difficulty, but the Frenchman was tardy in reacting to the emergency and her main topmast was carried away.

By 3 P.M., *Constellation* was ranging up on the lee quarter of the French ship. Her captain hailed Truxtun, but the latter refused to reply. Truxtun watched and waited while the range closed. "Why doesn't the Frenchman use his stern chasers?" he must have wondered.

Before we relive our ship's first great moment, and see a glorious battle distilled and made quaint by the filter of time, let us pause to remember what a sea battle between vessels of equal strength was really like in the heyday of fighting sail. Only hand-to-hand, face-to-face trench battles in the First World War could in any way compare to the horror of a sea fight. Each captain strove to bring his vessel close aboard in an advantageous position to his enemy in order to turn the enemy vessel into a splintered, burning matchbox. The business was slaughter! Men peered over cannon, through gunports, and saw the shot they fired at point-blank range tear men and boys to pieces. The masts rained canvas, blocks, tackle, line, and dagger-like splinters onto the weather decks, like trees shaking terrible fruit everywhere. Skulls were crushed, limbs broken, bodies impaled. Fires burned all around and men rushed madly about with leather buckets of water, slipping on blood while trying to put them out. At any moment your messmate's head might fly off, or his body disintegrate before your eyes. The young powder monkey running with shot to your gun, would suddenly fall as if tripped, only to see in amazement that his leg was no longer attached to his trunk. When "Stand by to repel boarders!" was called, or perhaps, "Boarders away," you grabbed a handy pike or boarding cutlass and rushed on deck to stab and hack at the nearest piece of enemy flesh on your ship or the foe's. If the match were even, you and your shipmates might count on a two-to-three-hour slaughter, with only a fifty-fifty chance of escaping with your life, and practically no chance of coming out of it unscathed. Officers had even less to hope for; their bright uniforms were the choice targets for the marine snipers in the tops and crosstrees. That was the glory of war at sea.

Standing by the great guns were Lieutenants Rodgers, Cowper, and Sterrett. When *Constellation* was almost atop of *L'Insurgente,* Truxtun answered the French skipper with one word: "Fire." The enemy returned the broadside and the melee was on. *Constellation's* first rounds swept the French frigate's quarterdeck, putting the battery of carronades out of action.

Broadside after broadside at almost point-blank range flew between the two maneuvering ships, the American part better handled, her adversary hampered by the downed main top. Their styles of battle were different. The French Navy, not wanting to destroy a valuable prize, sliced away at an opponent's top hamper, stripped her of canvas, rigging, shrouds, and masts, and made her helpless so that surrender would be the only reasonable outcome. For a Republican Navy, it was a most bourgeois method of fighting. Truxtun's experience and inclination caused him to adopt the British mode of sea battle: to hell with the prize—hull the enemy again and again, rip out her innards, smash the crew to pulp. Victory and glory, not a fat prize, were the objects of battle.

Finally, Truxton drove *Constellation* across the "T" and every gun on the starboard side of his ship came to bear individually on a line directly down the enemy's main deck. This was the knockout blow of old-fashioned naval warfare. The carnage on *L'Insurgente* was terrible to behold. At the same time *Constellation's* light guns in the tops and aft on the quarterdeck were shredding the Frenchman's top hamper.

The Constellation *engages* L'Insurgente   *February 9, 1799*

With a crew that outnumbered those on the American frigate, *L'Insurgente* prepared to board *Constellation,* but Captain Truxtun detected the maneuver, clapped on sail and easily widened the fifty yards that separated the two ships. As she drew away *Constellation* fired another broadside that raked *L'Insurgente* diagonally and then swung across her bow to deliver a second diagonal rake from the opposite side.

Although the Frenchman was in serious trouble, *Constellation* was not destined to get off unharmed, for at that moment an 18-pound ball from a gun mounted on *L'Insurgente's* forecastle struck *Constellation's* foremast just below the cap and left it in imminent danger of being carried away as the frigate rolled and pitched in the heavy sea. The midshipman of the foretop—an eighteen-year-old youngster named David Porter who was to make a name for himself in another war—saw the danger and hailed the quarterdeck for orders. When he found that he could not make his voice heard above the din of the battle, he raced up the shrouds, cut the slings of the topsail spar and lowered the yard to relieve the strain—a courageous act that prevented his ship from being disabled when victory was within her grasp.

Except for the damage to the mast, *Constellation* was relatively unscathed. On the quarterdeck of *L'Insurgente,* the wheel was unmanned, and Barreaut huddled with his lieutenants, obtaining their agreement that naught else could be done but surrender. So the French frigate struck her colors and the independent United States had won her first great naval victory.

Truxton's victory was remarkable not only for the skill with which he handled his ship, but also for the superb demonstration of American gunnery. *Constellation* carried twenty-eight long 24-pounders and ten long 12-pounders in this action, giving her a broadside weight of 396 pounds. *L'Insurgente,* according to Truxtun, carried twenty-four 12-pounders, two long 18-pounders, eight long 6-pounders, and four 36-pounders and two 24-pounder carronades, giving her a broadside of 282 pounds. As French shot were usually overwieght, one may add about twenty pounds to this figure. *Constellation's* crew numbered 309, *L'Insurgente's* 409, but this difference was of no importance as the Frenchmen were unable to board. There seems no doubt that the French ship was somewhat inferior to the American frigate and that the loss of her main topmast before the action placed her at a serious disadvantage. The French captain might have been under the impression that peace had been restored between the United States and France. He claimed that he was under orders from the Governor of Guadeloupe not to fire on American ships, although he had been taking American vessels all along.

Constellation's superior marksmanship played an important role.

The French had finally met "Yankee Racehorse." At least seventy of them were dead or wounded. American losses were one killed and three wounded. The only American officer injured was Midshipman James Macdonough, an older brother of Thomas Macdonough who was to win fame at the Battle of Plattsburgh in the War of 1812. He lost a foot while he was at his post in the maintop. Ironically, the only dead American, Seaman Neal Harvey, a gunner in one of Lt. Sterrett's crews, had been cut down by that officer when he broke in fright from his battle station. Truxtun logged the death of Harvey as "Killed in Action."

One of the three American wounded was a black seaman named William Brown, 60 years old, who was shot in the left foot by a musket ball fired from the enemy's tops. He recovered and continued to serve in *Constellation,* even after many of his shipmates accepted discharge stateside when the ship returned home. Brown saw action again in the encounter with *La Vengeance* and was discharged later that year. Most likely there were several black freemen serving on *Constellation.*

Constellation's "moment of truth" had been met and she had not been found wanting. The months of preparation and days of grinding drills had paid off. The chubby, ruddy-faced captain from Long Island, who had learned about battle at sea as a privateersman, and who knew the requirements of the officers and men aboard a man-of-war from his experience in the British Navy, had the satisfaction of seeing the vindication of his efforts to weld his own officers and men into a fighting unit that would be a model for the United States Navy. Truxtun had not written in vain his memoranda to his officers. Though they may have seemed harsh, they varied from a mild reprimand for slackness in attending to duties to scathing censures such as he addressed to Midshipman John Dent two weeks before the battle: "Was my own Son, who is in a similar Station with yourself in the Navy, to act as you have done, contrary to Example, and the most wholesome Advice, I should not only dismiss him the Service, but I believe I should disinherit, and let him shift for himself."

Truxtun's report to the Secretary of the Navy written on the run back to St. Christopher's is so laconic as to be almost smug. After detailing his movements from February 4 to the day of his encounter with *L'Insurgente,* he wrote:

. . .She hoisted American Colours and I made our private Signal for the Day, as well as that of the British, but finding she answered neither, must confess I immediately suspected her to be an Enemy, and in a short Time after found, that my Suspicions were well founded, for she hoisted the french national Colours, and fired a Gun to Windward (which is a Signal of an Enemy) I continued bearing down on her, and at ¼ past 3 PM she hailed me several Times, and as soon as I got in a Position for every Shot to do Execution I answered by commencing a close, and successful Engagement, which lasted untill about half after 4 PM, when she struck her Colours to the United States Ship, *Constellation,* and I immediately took possession of her; she proves to be the celebrated french national Frigage, *Insurgente* of 40 Guns, and 400 Men, lately out from France, commanded by Monsieur Barreaut, and is esteemed one of the fastest sailing Ships in the french Navy. I have been so much shattered in my Rigging and Sails, and my fore top Mast rendered from Wounds useless; you may depend the Enemy is not less so; I intend to get into Bassateer Roads, Saint Christophers if possible, with my Prize, but the Wind being adverse and blowing hard, I much doubt, in the crippled State of both Ships (without a Change) whether I shall effect it, and if not I must make a Port to Leeward. The high State of our Discipline, with the gallent conduct of all my Officers, and Men, would have enabled me to have compelled a more formidable Enemy to have yielded, had the Fortune of War thrown one in my Way; as it is, I hope the President and my Country will for the present be content, with a very fine Frigate being added to our infant Navy, and that too with the Loss of only one Man killed, and three wounded, while the Enemy had (the french Surgeon reports) Seventy killed, and wounded; several were found dead in her Tops, etc. and were thrown overboard, 18 Hours after we had Possesion of her. I must not omit in this hasty Detail to do Justice to Monsieur Barreaut for he defended his Ship manfully, and from my raking him several Times, fore and aft, and being, athwat his stem ready with every Gun to fire, when he struck his Colours, we may impute the Conflict not being more bloody on our Side, for had not these Advantages been taken, the Engagement would not have ended so soon, for the *Insurgent* was completely officered, and manned . . . P.S. Be pleased to write Mrs. Truxtun a line at Perth Amboy, and tell her I am well, for I have not Time. The *Insurgente* left Gaudelupe the 8th Instant having returned from a short Cruize a few days before, in which she took 5 valuable English ships, and got 4 of them Safe in, the Other the Captain says had not arrived when he sailed. The french Captain tells me, I have caused a War with France, if so I am glad of it, for I detest Things being done by Halves.

Truxtun makes no mention of the *L'Insurgente's* broken top mast and that she was therefore crippled when he engaged her. Also, he observes that while *L'Insurgente* was one of the best frigates in the French Navy, he could have done as well with even a better ship. It seems as if Truxtun would have been willing to take on a ship-of-the-line with *Constellation.*

A postscript to the engagement did not come to light for another quarter of a century when Charles W. Goldsborough, clerk of the Secretary of the Navy from 1798 to 1802, and Chief Clerk of the Navy Department from 1802 to 1813, gave details of the aftermath of the battle in an article in *The United States Naval Chronicle:*

> John Rodgers (Present Commodore Rodgers) first lieutenant, was sent with midshipman Porter (President captain D. Porter) and eleven men, to take possession of the prize, and superintend the removal of the crew to the *Constellation.* The wind blew high, and occasioned so much delay in removing the crew, that before it could be effected, night set in, and it came on to blow so hard as to separate the ships, leaving one hundred and seventy three prisoners on board *L'Insurgente,* to be guarded by Lieutenant Rodgers and his small party . . . The ordinary means of securing prisoners and the gratings having been thrown overboard by the crew of *L'Insurgente* soon after she struck, left Lieutenant Rodgers in a most embarrassing and perilous situation. *L'Insurgente* resembled a slaughter house; her decks not having been cleared of the dead or dying; her spars, sails, and rigging, cut to pieces, and lying on deck. The navigating her in this situation, in a gale of wind, by two officers and eleven men, who were at the same time charged with the duty of guarding one hundred and seventy three prisoners, without handcuffs or shackles, and hatches all uncovered, was a service not to be envied by the boldest man living . . . Under the circumstances, lieutenant Rodgers immediately secured all the small arms; Ordered the prisoners into the lower hold of the ship, and placed at each hatchway a sentinel, armed with a blunderbuss, cutlass, and brace of pistols, with orders to fire, if any one of the prisoners should attempt to come upon deck, without having previously obtained his permission. In this situation he was placed for three nights and two days, during which time, neither he nor midshipman Porter could take the slightest repose, being compelled to be constantly on the watch, to prevent the prisoners from rising upon them, and re-taking the ship, which their numbers would have enabled them to do, with ease, but for the precautions taken, and the vigilance practiced by lieutenant Rodgers and his party. One moment's intermission thereof would have lost the ship, as the prisoners had manifested a disposition to re-take her, and were incessantly on the watch for a favorable moment to accomplish their purpose. She was, under these circumstances, safely conducted into St. Kitts, at which place the *Constellation* had previously arrived.

When *Constellation* arrived with Captain Barreaut and many other French prisoners, followed by her prize, at Basseterre on February 13, she received an enthusiastic welcome from the British dignitaries. Captain Truxtun was particularly gratified by a personal request from his old friend Mr. Tyson, a member of the King's Council, that *Constellation* fire a salute so that it might be returned by His Majesty's forts. The British of course did not realize how much the American victory was a prediction of things to come. Lieutenant Rodgers made his official report of the killed and wounded on *L'Insurgente* and the latter were sent to the hospital ashore.

The United States Marines at this early stage in their history were generally regarded as necessary evils aboard ship. When Captain Truxtun wrote his report to the Secretary of the Navy of the engagement with *L'Insurgente* and commended his officers on their conduct, he neglected to mention Lieutenant Clinch and his marine detachment. Clinch was the first officer on *Constellation* to discover this omission when, while dining with the Captain a few days after the dispatches had been sent, Truxtun, in an expansive mood over their glass of wine, had his steward bring out the copy of the dispatch for the lieutenant to read. When Clinch asked him why his name had been omitted "the question seemed to embarass him for until that moment I am well convinced the omission had never occurred to him. He desired however that I would not feel uneasy and that any misconception would be removed when we arrived on the Continent." In his letter to the Commandant of the Marines, Clinch went on to say that when Truxtun distributed the swords surrendered by the French lieutenants on *L'Insurgente* to the lieutenants of *Constellation,* he was given the second best.

In a letter from Major (Commandant) William W. Burrows, United States Marine Corps, dated 19 February 1800, the Secretary of the Navy is requested to have the captains of ships provide separate chests for the marines' arms and cartridges, as was done in the British Navy, so that the men could get to quarters faster. It is also interesting to note that

Marine privates were paid four dollars less a month than ordinary seamen. As a result, several of *Constellation's* marines re-enlisted as ordinary seamen at the end of the cruise.

Truxtun now added *L'Insurgente*, tentatively renamed *Conquest*, to his squadron. *Constellation* was ready for sea before *L'Insurgente* and resumed her patrol on February 21. During the next two weeks she captured two small French privateers, *La Diligence* and *L'Union*, which were sent into port with prize crews. The work on *L'Insurgente* was not completed until the middle of March, and by transferring as many men as the other ships in his squadron could spare, Truxtun was able to supply her with about half her normal complement of hands, with Rodgers remaining in command.

Whatever other matters might have come to Truxtun's attention, those of *L'Insurgente* were never far from his mind. The flow of memos and orders from *Constellation* to Lieutenant Rodgers on *L'Insurgente* continued unabated and the commodore saw fit to give his personal attention to details that he must have known an officer of Rodger's ability could handle. A special code of signals between the two ships was drawn up and white flag flown from the main was prescribed as *L'Insurgente's* private signal. Rodgers was repeatedly warned against running any risks whatever; he was always to keep a good lookout at night and always be on his guard against attack, and when he returned to the roads after filling his water casks, he was to anchor "in a good Burth not too far out, nor too far in Shore." Truxtun was determined that nothing should happen to his prize before she was delivered to his admiring countrymen in Hampton Roads. She was the first ship captured by an American man-of-war and he considered her "one of the best calculated frigates, now under our Flag, for the Present War."

By March 11, the work on *L'Insurgente* had been finished, and as it was evident that no more could be recruited in the area to complete her complement, Truxtun decided to find Commodore Barry's squadron and ask for the loan of some of his seamen. The two frigates left Basseterre at 8 A.M., and cruised southward until Guadeloupe was abeam at noon of

the following day. Wishing to have a look at what might be at
anchor there, *Constellation* beat up toward the harbor while
L'Insurgente remained at a safe distance.

At 6 A.M. on the morning of the 14th, when only three
leagues from port, *Constellation* met and took the French
letter-of-marque schooner renamed *L'Union*, armed with six
guns and carrying a cargo of dry goods and provisions. A
prize crew headed by Lieutenant John Archer was put aboard
and the three ships hovered off the French stronghold for the
remainder of the day, while *Constellation* and *L'Insurgente*
spoke two other vessels that proved to be of British and
Danish registry. As Commodore Barry's squadron did not
seem to be in the area, the two frigates headed for St. Kitts
with their prize.

Having heard that three French privateers had been
sighted in the area, Truxtun then decided to sail with the convoy as far as Eustatia where he hoped he might find them.
The fleet sailed at 4 P.M., March 21, with the ship *George
Washington*, under Captain Patrick Fletcher, and the brig
Pickering, under Captain Joseph Ingraham, as escorts for the
merchant men, with *Constellation* bringing up the rear. After
chasing a sail to the west of St. Bartholomew that ran so
close to the island that he could not follow, Truxtun sailed
past the port of Gustavis to see what lay in the harbor. A
French privateer was visible, but as St. Bartholomew was
neutral (Swedish), he had to content himself with cruising
outside for an hour or two before proceeding to windward.

On March 22, an incident demonstrated the delicacy of the
position the United States Government had assumed in
limiting the prizes its ships could take to those of French
registry, while permitting other ships to pass even though
they were engaged in trade with the French and carried
French cargoes. At 5:30 A.M., a ship and schooner were
sighted, and *Constellation* went after the former, which proved to be HM Frigate *Padri*. Courtesies were exchanged, and
Constellation departed to chase the schooner, which was
overtaken and stopped some two hours later. On examining
her papers she was found to be the Swedish schooner *Active*,
bound for St. Bartholomew from Guadeloupe, and was per-

mitted to proceed. Almost immediately *Padrie* brought her to and seized her as a prize. Although a seaman from *L'Insurgente*, who had agreed to serve on *Constellation*, told Truxtun that *Active* belonged to a Frenchman in Guadeloupe, Truxtun felt his orders did not permit him to delay her and collect the prize money she would have brought.

On his return to St. Kitts on March 24, Captain Truxtun found that the long awaited *Baltimore* and a store ship had arrived, and *Richmond* and the cutter *Virginia* had returned to port. The next three days were occupied with unloading the store ship and stowing the supplies she had brought in, attending to the details of the ship's keeping, and making plans for the future operations of the squadron. Lieutenant Samuel Barron, who had been promoted to captain although his new commission had not yet arrived, was given command of the *Baltimore*.

After several unproductive patrols under Lieutenant Rodgers, *L'Insurgente* joined *Constellation* at Basseterre and the two frigates sailed for the United States in the latter part of April. The enlistments of the men of *Constellation* had expired and it was time to take them home. On May 20, *Constellation* and *L'Insurgente* came to anchor in Hampton Roads, the latter flying the French Tricolor below the Stars and Stripes on her gaff.

The news of the capture "of the first governmental ship of any consequence ever made by the arms of the United States, at sea, since our being known as a nation" was received with enthusiasm in the United States. The thanks of the President to Captain Truxtun and the officers and men of *Constellation* "for their good conduct and gallantry on this occasion" were expressed in a letter from Secretary of the Navy Stoddert dated March 13:

> The President desires me to communicate to you, his high approbation of the whole of your able and judicious conduct in the West Indies; and to Present to you, and through you, to the officers and men of the *Constellation*, his thanks for the good conduct, exact discipline, and bravery displayed in the action with, and capture of, the French frigate *Insurgente*, on the 9th February. I must, however, add, that he observes, and all the officers of the government, indeed all others I have heard speak on the subject, join me in this observation, that this is nothing but what we expected from Truxtun.

In commemoration of the victory Captain Truxtun presented his officers with the swords of the captured French lieutenants, and Lloyd's of London awarded him a silver urn. An obscure engraver named E. Savage, who lived in Philadelphia and who had just discovered a method of engraving copper plates with acid, was inspired to execute two aquatints of the battle for ex-President Washington, which were the first such prints to be made in the United States and are now among the rarest of collector's items.

Captain Truxtun, the victorious *Constellation,* and the vanquished *L'Insurgente* received an enthusiastic welcome at Norfolk, and the men whose enlistments had expired were paid off. According to Carpenter's mate John Hoxse, "the greater part of his old hands" accepted Captain Truxtun's offer of "a beaver hat and black silk handkerchief, two months'advance pay, and two weeks' liberty on shore" if they would re-enlist. They did, and *Constellation* proceeded from Hampton Roads to New York in the latter part of June for refitting.

Truxtun felt his ship's guns were too heavy and the ship heeled too radically under a breeze with 24's on her deck, so he struck them in favor of 18's. Also he supplanted the long 12's on her quarterdeck with 32 pounder carronades he had liked on *L'Insurgente.* Thus he shifted *Constellation's* center of gravity while maintaining the weight of her broadside. This change made *Constellation* in effect more a "cruiser" and less of a "battleship."

There was prize money coming to all hands, many of whom served for the sake of it, for their pay was not enough on which to live. An Admiralty Court judged the prize, and the laws were tricky. If the prize vessel were judged superior to the winning ship, the value belonged entirely to the crew. If the taken ship were inferior, the government received half the value. *L'Insurgente* was judged superior, and the men were able to cash in their prize tickets. What a shame that while the officers received their shares, most of the seamen and marines had sold their tickets beforehand to speculators for a portion of their value, or lost them, or simply never bothered to collect their hard-earned money.

Constellation was the darling of New York and her sailors each had the key to the heart of the city. All day long small boats beat out to the harbor to circle the conquering eagle, anchored near Staten island. Excursions were run from the Battery, and the fashionable ladies and gentlemen of New York City risked their finery in the salt spray to see the mighty ship. Many songs were penned in celebration. Among the most popular was THE CONSTELLATION AND THE INSURGENTE. The first two stanzas follow:

> Come all ye Yankee sailors, with swords and pikes advance,
> 'Tis time to try your courage and humble haughty Francy,
> > The sons of France our seas invade,
> > Destroy our commerce and our trade,
> > 'Tis time the reck'ning should be paid!
> > > To brave Yankee boys.
>
> On board the *Constellation,* from Baltimore we came,
> We had a bold commander and Truxtun was his name!
> > Our ship she mounted forty guns,
> > And on the main so swiftly runs,
> > To prove to France Columbia's sons,
> > > Are brave Yankee boys.

Captain Truxtun departed for Perth Amboy to visit the home he had not seen for nine months and the wife to whom he had said "good bye" in Philadelphia the previous December.

Arrangements were made for him to keep in close touch with his frigate, and when he learned that the New York Health Department had complained to the Secretary of the Navy that its physician had reported sickness aboard *Constellation* and that the officer in charge had been careless about communication with the shore, he called on his surgeon, Dr. Isaac Henry, for a report. He advised the doctor to see that both the sick men who were aboard and those who had been sent to the hospital ashore "must be fed with greens and fresh meat." His ship and his men were never far from his mind.

Then, suddenly and without warning, like a spark in a powder magazine, Truxtun, on August 1, 1799, resigned his commission.

A Show Of Force

His Crew, the Navy, the Government, and the Country recoiled from the shock of Captain Truxtun's resignation. The nation's great hero of the moment was leaving the service. Why?

On hearing the unexpected news that Captain Silas Talbot had been restored to the list of Navy captains, still ahead of him, Truxton concluded that he had been passed over unjustly, and his pride triggered an immediate resignation. Though Talbot had been Truxtun's senior on the original list of 1794, his frigate had not been completed. Truxtun probably did not think more than a few minutes about his decision before he made it. After all, Talbot had left the Navy for the merchant service and was making money while Truxtun served his country. President John Adams had made an error and the Navy was in jeopardy of losing its very best captain.

The saddened ship bid the commander farewell, expecting never to see him again.

As *Constellation* was nearly ready for sea, Captain Samuel Barron was ordered to assume command on August 13, 1799, and take her out in search of a 44-gun French frigate which Master Commandant William Bainbridge had reported northbound off the Florida Keys. Barron sailed as far north as St. Mary's River in Georgia, without finding the enemy or speaking to a ship that had sighted her, before reversing his course and returning to New York in the middle of September.

Orders were then received to provision *Constellation* for a six month cruise; but as the "fever" was raging in New York and supplies were short, the orders were changed to a six week cruise back to St. Mary's River to patrol the southern coast until November 10, when she was to report in at Hampton Roads. A list of the supplies needed for the projected cruise was to be forwarded to the Navy agent in Norfolk so that there would be no delay in that port.

Captain Truxtun's resignation had been received with regret by the Secretary of the Navy, and he urged Truxtun to reconsider. *Constellation's* lieutenants, purser, and surgeon expressed their sorrow and "acknowledgement and grateful thanks for the kind & Paternal Care you have uniformly exercised toward us." Truxtun replied with a letter of appreciation that concluded with his usual homily about duty, love of country, and attention to order in the ship.

Truxtun did not really want to leave the service. After all, he had had command of the finest frigate in the Western Hemisphere. He had built *Constellation,* manned her, trained her crew, fashioned them into a magnificent fighting team, and wielded a will for victory in them. He knew every beam, every nail, and every peg of the great young ship. His body and her deck moved as one. Sometimes she had seemed to heel, to pitch, to turn, to tack, and to run before the wind almost without orders and human effort, as if in response to the yet unspoken commands of his mind. Was all this, and the hope of greater glory to be lost for the sake of pride?

His influential friend, Charles Biddle, appealed to him; Secretary of the Navy Stoddert again asked him to reconsider. Finally, old General Washington, always the best friend to the Navy, asked *Constellation's* former commander to visit Mount Vernon on September 12, 1799.

Fortunately, compromise was reached. Truxtun agreed to withdraw his resignation if he would never have to serve under Talbot. On October 23, 1799, the Secretary of the Navy wrote:

I have now the pleasure to return your commission by order of the President. It has never been accepted by him or there would have been insurmountable difficulties in the way of restoring you to the rank you held in 1794. You must be satisfied to submit to the arrangements of that year and must rely upon the desire which the President feels and which will continue to be felt by the Officer at the head of this Department whoever he may be to save your feelings from unnecessary mortification, without entering into any stipulation, which is indeed impossible, as you will readily see on a little reflection.

It is intended if agreeable to yourself, that you should resume the command of the *Constellation* at Norfolk, where she will be the 10th of Novr, & that you will proceed to your old station where you will have command of a considerable part of our Force—Captn Barry is going to France, & Captain Talbott has his station at Saint Domingo—I wish to hear from you as quickly as possible, for it is time that I should make arrangments for the *Constellation* should you not take her.

Some doubt of Captain Truxtun's being able to accept the assignment arose when he developed an indisposition while still at home in Perth Amboy. On October 28, the Secretary of the Navy wrote that he was sorry to hear that Truxton was ill and that he would delay making other arrangements until he had further word on the captain's health. A convoy for the Mississippi was being collected in Norfolk and plans had been made to have *Constellation* act as escort as far as the Gulf of Mexico. General Wilkinson, a former aide of Benedict Arnold (and future conspirator), was aboard one of the ships bound New Orleans on an important mission. Truxtun was advised that if his health would permit him to join *Constellation* in Norfolk by November 20, the sailing of the convoy would be delayed until that date; otherwise it would have to leave with only a 12-gun schooner as escort and he would be ordered to complete the fitting out of the new 44-gun frigate *(President)* nearing completion in New York. If he joined *Constellation,* Truxtun was told that he would have the following vessels under his command in the West Indies: the 44-gun *John Adams;* the 24-gun *Connecticut,* the 32-gun *Adams,* the 14-gun *Pickering,* the 14-gun *Eagle,* the 20-gun *Delaware,* and the 20-gun *Baltimore.*

On November 6, Captain Barron was advised that Truxtun would relieve him on *Constellation* and that he would take over the completion of *Chesapeake.* On November 11, the Secretary addressed his final detailed orders to Captain Truxtun aboard *Constellation.*

Constellation's departure was delayed by the difficulty of chartering and loading a store ship to accompany her to St. Kitts, where the squadron was badly in need of supplies. It was not until December 24 that she was able to get under way. By 3 P.M. on Christmas Day, the pilot had been discharged, Cape Henry light bore northwest by west—four leagues distant—and the frigate was settling back into her sea routine with Captain Truxtun again in command.

The voyage back to the West Indies was delayed by foul weather, unexpectedly strong currents, and the slowness of the store ship. On January 5, Truxtun noted that "The numerous colds & coughs with which the crew were effected, for a considerable time before we sailed from the Chesapeake—begin to suside [sic] fast—and by the Surgeons Report this day only ten remained in his list, and Six of these are under Veneral complaints, of long standing, thus we may call the Ship Remarkably healthy . . . Employed repairing of Sails, that have been much injured by rats—and unhanging the port lids, as I find the Ship very Stiff in compari (s) on to what she was with 24 p^d cannon on her decks— and these lids with their hinges & Iron work, I calculate each 4 C^{wt} which takes from the Sides of the Ship Six tons weight."

A landfall was finally made on Antigua on January 19, and *Constellation* let go her anchor in the Basseterre Roads at 7 o'clock the following evening.

The American men-of-war lying in the Basseterre Roadstead were ordered to get under way at once and proceed to their assigned sectors, where they were to stay until forced to return to the rendezvous for supplies and fresh water. Truxtun lost no time in getting his own frigate ready to follow them to sea. French privateers would not be taken nor new laurels won by ships that loitered in port. The dynamic new commodore of the St. Kitts station was determined to carry out Secretary Stoddert's orders that the ships of his squadron were to be kept "constantly cruising."

While *Constellation* was preparing for sea, a vessel arrived from the United States with the news that George Washington had died on December 14. As directed in a general order from the Navy Department, the flags of all the ships of the squadron were ordered flown at half-mast for one week. The commissioned officers had a band of black crepe sewn on their left sleeves below the elbow which they were to wear for six months.

Seaward went the *Adams, John Adams, Baltimore, Eagle,* and *Pickering.* Truxtun dispatched *Eagle* to find *Enterprize* for a special mission he had in mind. Dispatches for the Secretary of the Navy were forwarded, and when news was brought aboard that a 44-gun French frigate and a 28-gun corvette were at Guadeloupe, preparations were hurried to get underway.

After only nine days in port, *Constellation* shoved off at 4 P.M. January 30, and stood to windward. Early the next morning *L'Insurgente* was sighted with a convoy, and Truxtun went aboard to examine her damaged foremast. At 11 A.M. the frigates parted.

Where were the Frenchmen? Truxtun and *Constellation* wanted another crack at them. The cocky captain had ordered a large hold cleared of all gear by the carpenter in order to accommodate some five hundred prisoners he hoped to have aboard in a few days.

At half past seven in the morning of February 1, while she was still several leagues from the French stronghold, *Constellation's* lookout sighted a large ship on the southeastern horizon. Although a French frigate had been reported at Guadeloupe, Truxtun's first thought on seeing the stranger so far to the south of the island and steering westward was that she was a Britisher, probably out of Martinique and headed for Jamaica. As a long sail to leeward would be required to overtake her, he had the English colors hoisted hoping that she would come about and meet him halfway. When no answering signal was displayed and the stranger showed no inclination to speak, Truxtun became suspicious and ordered every sail set on *Constellation* to give chase.

With the wind on her quarter *Constellation* gained rapidly. By mid-morning the officers on her quarterdeck were able to identify their quarry by her soft, graceful lines as a French warship of perhaps fifty-four guns. Imagine—a fifty-four running from a thirty-eight! The size and armament of the enemy vessel bordered on that of a third-rate ship-of-the-line. Did the French fear they had met up with the dreaded Yankee Racehorse?

Captain Truxtun immediately ordered his ship cleared for action and the crew sent to battle stations. To make his frigate more maneuverable if the enemy decided to alter course and accept battle, he had bag reefs taken in the topsails and the yards slung with chains so they would be less vulnerable to bar and chain shot. As a final precaution, he reinforced with stoppers the lines controlling the sails that would be kept set during battle. To make it clear to the enemy that he meant to engage her, Truxtun ordered the British ensign lowered and the Stars and Stripes hoisted to the gaff. On deck the Americans roared their pride and approval. Here was a worthy opponent for *Constellation,* the finest man-of-war in the Caribbean; but, they had a long haul ahead before they could hope to catch the fast-sailing adversary.

The men of *Constellation* would not know for another two months that they were taking on the French frigate *La Vengeance,* under Captain F.M. Pitot.

At noon the wind became light and the French frigate pulled ahead, but Truxtun was determined to continue the chase even though it took him further from his cruising ground and he would lose valuable time if he was unsuccessful. His doggedness was rewarded within an hour by a freshening of the wind, and from one o'clock until eight o'clock that evening *Constellation* bore steadily down on her opponent. When the two frigates were close enough for a hail to be heard, Truxtun ordered the candles in his battle lanterns lighted and he took his position in the lee gangway to demand the Frenchman's surrender. Resting the heavy speaking trumpet on the rail, he was about to shout his ultimatum across the darkened waters when the French frigate opened fire with stern chasers and quarter guns, and shot whistled through his rigging.

The Constellation *battles* La Vengeance *at night off Guadaloupe February 1, 1800*

This was the moment for which Captain Truxtun had been waiting and the opportunity that he had hoped would be his when he accepted the rank of fifth on the list of captains in the United States Navy, though he believed he should have been third. Tossing the speaking trumpet aside, he ordered the helmsman to hold his course and then dispatched Midshipman Vandyke to the gun deck to warn the officers commanding the gun divisions "not to throw away a single charge of powder and shot, but to take good aim, and to fire directly into the hull of the enemy, and to load principally with two round shot, and now and then with a round shot and a stand of grape."

As *Constellation* drew up on her opponent Lieutenant Sterett's guns in the forward division were the first to bear and were fired exactly as Captain Truxtun had ordered. Before Sterett had time to reload, Lieutenant Shirley's division had the French frigate in their sights. The double shot in each of his 18-pounders crashed into the enemy's planking between wind and water, and gun after gun in *Constellation's* larboard broadside went into action. The men at the carronades on the spar deck fired and reloaded with the same deliberation as those at the great guns below them, while the marines in the tops maintained a steady fire directed at the men exposed on the French frigate's topsides. The enemy's deck turned red as men were crushed with cannon balls, pierced with splinters, and knocked down by musket shot. Americans were dying too, though fewer in number.

With *Constellation* maintaining the weather gauge, the two ships ran side by side, battling in the moonlight for nearly five hours, pouring broadside after broadside into each other at a range of less than five hundred yards. The American frigate's fire was returned furiously for the first half hour of the engagement and her head sails were carried away, but when Captain Truxtun ordered his ship to fall off until the damage could be repaired, his opponent crowded on more sail and attempted to escape. Within a few minutes *Constellation* was back abreast of her enemy and her guns resumed their deliberate fire. On at least two occasions Truxtun attempted to get his ship into position to rake, but each time his movements were anticipated and his efforts foiled by the French captain's adroit maneuvering.

Shortly before one o'clock, as the moon went down, the French frigate's few remaining operative guns ceased firing, and she attempted to sheer off. Truxtun did not realize it for the noise and darkness, but Captain Pitot had at least twice struck his colors in surrender. As the French vessel turned, Captain Truxtun ordered his shattered sails trimmed to lay *Constellation* alongside so that boarders could be called away if she did not surrender. Before the order could be carried out, word was passed to him that all of the main mast's shrouds and braces had been shot away and it was in danger of going over the side. A quick glance convinced Truxtun that the rigging was cut in so many places that stoppers would be useless, and his only chance of saving the mast was to get new braces on it as soon as possible. With the security of his ship at stake, any thought of boarding the enemy frigate and taking a prize was abandoned while all hands were called from the gun deck to help rig temporary stays and brace the mast.

Midshipman James Jarvis, in charge of the main top—a key post—was warned by one of his men that the mast was about to give way and that they had better get down. But as Captain Truxtun remarked in his report of the action, Jarvis "had already so much the principle of an officer engrafted on his mind, not to leave his quarters, that he replied, if the mast went, they must go with it." Unfortunately the emergency had been discovered too late and before the topmen could be called down or a single brace hauled taut, the mast broke off just above the level of the deck and crashed over the side, carrying the mizzen topmast with it and hurling the topmen into the water. Only one man was saved. Jarvis was never seen again.

With his ship disabled by the mast dragging over the side and its wreckage strewing the deck, Truxtun's first concern was to get the debris cleared away in case his late opponent should decide to return and resume the battle. A full hour was required to complete the task and when it was finished the French frigate had disappeared in the darkness, perhaps sunk. Pursuit was out of the question and, as it would have been impossible for *Constellation* to beat up to windward to return to St. Kitts, a course was shaped for the island of Jamaica, some seven hundred miles to the westward.

Constellation's company spent the remaining hours of darkness assessing the damage and making her as seaworthy as possible. The crippled foremast was secured and a foresail and foretopsail at half-mast were set to give the ship steering way. A quick inspection revealed that she did "not have a spar or a fathom of rigging abaft the foremast," but that although the hull was "very much battered," it had suffered no serious damage below the waterline. When casulties were counted it was found that thirteen of the crew, as well as Midshipman Jarvis, had been killed in action and that Surgeon Isaac Henry was caring for twenty-six wounded sailors and marines in the cockpit.

A welcome ration of spirits was issued at daybreak and breakfast was eaten by the ship's weary company as soon as the galley fires could be lighted; all hands then turned to rig a mizzen stay-sail from the stump of the main mast to the head of the mizzenmast and to reinforce the braces of the latter to permit the setting of more aftersail. Throughout the daylight hours the work of cleaning up after a battle was continued and by nightfall a semblance of order had been restored.

On the following day, February 3, the 12-gun schooner *Enterprize,* under the command of Lieutenant John Shaw—and with Captain Truxtun's midshipman son on board—was ordered back to the United States with the reports of the battle.

Truxtun sent a terse dispatch to the Secretary of the Navy that hinted at the events of the previous day. After detailing his activities at St. Kitts and mentioning his meeting with *L'Insurgente,* Truxtun continued: "At half past seven A.M. of the following day, I discovered a sail to the southeast to which I gave chase; and for the further particulars of that chase, and the action after it, I must beg leave to refer you to the extracts from my journal, which is inclosed, as being the best mode of exhibiting a just, fair, and candid account of all our transactions in the late business, which had ended in the complete dismantlement of the *Constellation,* though I trust to the high reputation of the American flag . . ."

In a subsequent report to the Secretary of the Navy, Truxtun said he was convinced that "the French ship of war *La Vengeance* had struck to me, and was my prize," but because of the loss of his main mast he was unable to take her and she made off in the darkness, "the moon having gone down about 1 A.M." He likened *La Vengeance's* escape to that of *Santa Anna,* which had fled from Nelson's fleet at Trafalgar after she had struck her colors. The weather was very hazy when daylight came and he was unable to sight *La Vengeance.* Truxtun quotes Lieutenant Robertson who was in charge of some of the carronades on the quarterdeck: "I can not, sir bring the carronades to bear"; they were then on *La Vengeance's* weather quarter, "not half a pistol shot off." Truxtun said: "Never mind, Robertson, she is all our own, we have nothing to do but get alongside of her." Then the mainmast went over the side.

A "Gentleman" who was on board *Constellation* at the time wrote an account of the battle which is substantially the same as Truxtun's, but with some interesting additions. He says that when Truxtun's orders were received on the gun deck "At last the gallant (Lieutenant) Sterett got his bow gun to bear, and he played him well. We soon got the weather gage of him, and returned the civility with the candor and integrity that the sons of Columbia will I hope ever be remarkable for, in defence of their country's flag . . . As to the enemy there is not a doubt of his being sunk. As we had the weather gage he was completely hulled, and must have received many shot between wind and water; he had three ports knocked in one; his bowsprit and fore and main topmasts carried away, and as he was double manned the carnage must have been great. They seemed in great distress at quitting us; their pumps were going, at 4 o'clock signal guns were heard from them, and shortly after she disappeared." In an earlier paragraph he states that when they were coming up on the chase and were about to hail her, they heard someone say (in French), "She's but a Yankee frigate, and we'll board him."

Claypoole's American Daily Advertiser of Philadelphia dated April 28, 1800, gave official comparison of the strength of *Constellation* vs. *La Vengeance*. According to report *Constellation* mounted twenty-eight 18-pounders on the gun deck and ten 24-pounder carronades on the upper or spar deck to give her a total weight in metal of one round of 744 pounds. *La Vengeance* mounted thirty-two French 18-pounders (which Truxtun claimed carried a ball of English weight twenty pounds) on the gun deck, fourteen French 12-pounders (carrying a ball of thirteen and one-half English pounds) on her upper deck, and an additional eight carronades of thirty-six pounds French, equal to forty-two pounds English, for a total discharge of one round of 1165 pounds. A broadside would be only half of these weights. *Constellation* had 320 officers and men aboard; *La Veangeance* had 500 officers and crew, and 60 troops and passengers.

The casualties on *La Vengeance* probably numbered about one hundred, although estimates were as high as one hundred sixty. The French vessel had been hulled over two hundred times and was saved from sinking only by the American prisoners who manned her pumps, and who were as eager to save themselves as the French crew. Many would be wounded and would have no chance to survive in the sea. A translation of a certificate given each of the prisoners by Captain Pitot stated that he had demanded to be put and had remained below decks during the action, and that after the action was over had "wrought with all possible zeal and activity in repairing the damage which this frigate sustained." The certificate concluded with the request that, in view of the prioner's cooperation in saving *La Vengeance,* no French naval officer or privateersman interfere with or molest him on his return to the United States.

Three days after the battle, *La Vengeance* made her way into the neutral port of Curacao, where her crew attempted to assess and repair the damage. Captain Thomas Baker of the U.S. Frigate *Delaware,* which was in the harbor at the time for the purpose of refilling her water casks, made discrete inquiries and learned that her commanding officer, Captain Pitot, had told the governor of the island that he had been in an engagement with an unidentified British or American ship-of-the-line that mounted sixty guns and carried a crew of five hundred officers and men. In his report to the Secretary of the Navy, Captain Baker noted that only *La Vengeance's* bowsprit, fore and mizzen masts were standing, that her fore and mizzen shrouds and ratlines were so cut up that one could scarce see any of them for stoppers, that her starboard side was pocked with shot holes, and that she had eight feet of water in her hold. Reports of her casualties varied from twenty to fifty killed and forty to one hundred ten wounded.

A letter from a "Gentleman" in Curacao when *La Vengeance* arrived, was reprinted in *The Massachusetts Mercury* of Boston on August 19, 1800. After describing the condition of the ship, he noted that she was so badly damaged that "she was purposely run on shore to the windward of the port to secure her entrance into that place." Among the passengers were Generals Pellardie and LaGrande with a number of artillery officers, "which enabled the commander to station at least one to each gun" during the battle. Captain Pettot [sic] spoke in high terms of the conduct and gallantry of his adversary and described the vivid fire from the *Constellation* as superior to any thing he had ever seen (his own words were 'Superbe et Grande') and he mentioned when the flying jib boom of the *Constellation* ran into his mizzen shrouds, he supposed his adversary intended to board, and he called his men upon the upper deck, at which moment he received a shower of grape. Pitot assumed that he had engaged an English ship "of two complete batteries." A footnote says: "He supposed it an English vessel, and yet attempted to avoid an action for fear of shedding *American blood*. A very good story indeed."

From letters and reports written from Curacao it was learned that *La Vengeance* had left Guadeloupe for France on January 31, with a crew of 320 men. Thirty-six were impressed American seamen, and the sixty passengers included two French generals and a number of artillery officers. During the battle the passengers had been mustered at quarters and had helped fight, but the Americans had been permitted to remain below decks. One of the frigate's lieutenants stated that she had struck her colors at least twice and probably three times during the engagement, but her signal of surrender had apparently not been seen by her opponent and she had continued to fight until the stranger's mainmast went over the side and she had been able to escape in the darkness.

Pitot later faced a court-martial, and resorted to downright lies as well as exaggerations to excuse his failure. He inadvertantly paid Truxtun and *Constellation* a great compliment saying "The ship we fought is a ship of the line . . ." His report also made excuses for his running initially, apologized for the lack of readiness of his crew, and claimed he was undermanned. He explained that he had to station military passengers with the gun crew, and said his men were weary, but ultimately he claimed "victory to the flag of the Republic."

Just what had been accomplished? Tactically, an American frigate had defeated, but failed to capture, a larger French warship. Strategically, the Caribbean waters were safer for American shipping. Diplomatically, American negotiations with the French government were strengthened. Most importantly, however, it had been shown that the victory over *L'Insurgente* was no fluke. American shipbuilding, seamanship, and gunnery—products of a nation under thirty years of age—were at least equal qualitatively to those of one of the two greatest world powers. In the near term, it would be these two engagements of the *Constellation* with the French that would herald the victories of American naval arms in the War of 1812. The high morale and the tradition of victory of the United States Navy were established forever.

Caribbean Tour

On the morning after the action with *La Vengeance* Captain Truxtun formally thanked his officers and men. He was answered by an address signed by Lieutenant Sterett for the sea lieutenants, Lieutenant Clinch for the Marines, and the warrant officers and two petty officers for the crew. It was "well done!" for all hands this time.

On February 4, 1800, *L'Insurgente* hove in sight and was directed to accompany her conqueror to Jamaica, where the two frigates came to anchor on February 8. Finding that a new main mast could not be obtained in Jamaica, Captain Truxtun set up a jury rig and sailed for Norfolk on March 1. The details of the temporary repairs are unknown but they must have been gems of seamanship and Yankee ingenuity, for when *Constellation* departed from Port Royal she was capable of taking a convoy of fourteen merchantmen under her wing for the voyage home. Her log contains numerous entries of her beating to windward and of weathering several violent squalls.

Truxtun's report of the engagement was delivered to the Secretary of the Navy on February 23, and when *Constellation* sailed into Hampton Roads in the last week of March, Norfolk was ready with another round of dinners and a gala reception for her captain and his crew. Although a few discordant notes were heard from the Republican opposition in Congress, the House voted March 29, 1800, to have struck for Truxtun a "golden medal, emblematical of the late action between the United States Frigate *Constellation,* of thirty-eight guns, and the French ship of war *La Vengeance,* of fifty-four" to commemorate a battle that was "honourable to the American name, and instructive to its rising navy." After little debate Congress also passed a resolution that "the conduct of James Jarvis, a Midshipman in said frigate, who gloriously preferred certain death to an abandonment of his post, is deserving of the highest praise, and that the loss of so promising an officer is a subject of national regret." Next day the President ordered Secretary of the Navy to have the medal made, but Truxtun did not actually receive it for two years.

Truxtun's Medal

Secretary Stoddert requested Congress to create the rank of admiral for his friend, but the proposed act died in committee and he had to be content with promoting Truxtun to the command of the larger frigate *President,* which had just been launched in New York. The United States Navy would not have its first admiral until Farragut, over sixty years after Stoddert recommended Truxtun's name to Congress.

These events signalled a tragic turn in Truxtun's fortunes, for the Commodore's last twenty-two years were full of disappointment and bitterness. When he died in 1822, he was laid to rest near other great Americans of the early Republic in Christ Church cemetery, Philadelphia. At the time his most apt pupil, the former first lieutenant of *Constellation,* Commodore John Rodgers, was crowning a glorious naval career as senior officer of the United States Navy.

The turning point came soon after Thomas Truxtun arrived in Hampton Roads and moved *Constellation* up the Elizabeth River to the Navy Yard. Naval Constructor Josiah Fox was supplied with a list of the spars and repairs that she would need. When Fox pointed out that the Yard was already working to capacity building *Chesapeake* and repairing *Congress,* Captain Truxtun took advantage of his position as senior officer present and issued an order that the refitting of *Constellation* was to have top priority. Truxtun expected his orders to be obeyed immediately, just as at sea.

Now it was the turn of the usually cautious and circumspect Secretary Stoddert to make a slip. Thinking of Truxtun's great potential, Stoddert wrote to him that he should act as if "you were already an Admiral . . . or as if you had Command of the whole Navy." It was a disastrous thing to say to a man like Truxtun! For he did just that, taking over the entire Navy, referring to himself as "Commander in Chief of the Navy of the U.S." He tried to strip his best officers from *Constellation* and ship them on board *President.* That would have been fine for him, but tough for his successor. Stoddert said no to this.

While repairs were in progress, Captain Alexander Murray replaced Truxtun in command of *Constellation,* and by the middle of May she was again ready for sea. Captain Truxtun ordered Captain Murray to join Commodore Barry's squadron on the St. Kitts station where the frigate had been based on her two previous tours of duty in the Caribbean. On the day before he departed from Norfolk, Murray wrote a note to Secretary Stoddert, mentioning his destination, and commending "the Zeal of our Worthy Commodore." The Navy Department had intended to send *Constellation* to the Santo Domingo station some five hundred miles to the west of St. Kitts, and when Murray's letter was received the Secretary let Captain Truxtun know that the assignment of the ships of the United States Navy was a prerogative of the President. Truxtun's action "was in every way improper."

Meanwhile, Captain Murray was very pleased indeed with the ship for she was a sharply honed fighting machine. The new skipper had been a merchant sailor, a Revolutionary War soldier, a privateersman and a lieutenant in the Continental Navy.

Constellation had sailed from Hampton Roads on May 20, and before the pilot was dropped Captain Murray wrote to Stoddert reporting that they had finally gotten underway, after "having been detained 4 days for want of a fair Wind and much interrupted by continual bad weather for some time past." The pilot also carried a thank-you letter to Truxtun. Murray was a competent commander and a decent man. He was not, however, to be very lucky with his new ship.

Constellation's voyage back to the Caribbean was slowed by head winds and required an entire month. A few days out, one of the seamen reported sick with small pox and twenty-five of the crew were inoculated—one died. Only American vessels were met and none had intelligence of any enemy in the area. After a turn around Guadeloupe, Murray headed his frigate towards Basseterre, St. Kitts, to see if *Chesapeake* had arrived. He then planned on running over to Cayenne or Curacao, as he was anxious to keep an eye on *La Vengeance* in the latter port. How *Constellation's* crew ached to take on the French once more and administer the *coupe de grace*. *Constellation* arrived at Basseterre on June 21, 1800, and within a few days was back on her former cruising ground.

On June 26, *Constellation* recaptured the ship *Minerva* of

Peperelborough, near Guadeloupe. Midshipman Joshua Herbert was put in command and ordered to proceed to St. Kitts where he was to await a northbound convoy. A week later Midshipman James Cox was given command of the prize schooner *Greyhound* with orders to take her to St. Kitts. Manning these prizes weakened *Constellation's* crew considerably, and First Lieutenant Bartholomew Clinch was notified that some of his marines would have to serve the guns in the frigate's batteries.

At midnight on July 2, two vessels were sighted and chased. The schooner overtaken was *Charming Betsy,* which had been captured by a French privateer. She was boarded and it was "found she appeared under Danish papers" but the French prize master denied this. *Charming Betsy* had no log book or journal to clear up the "intricacy of the affair." On arriving at Martinique, the captain wanted Murray to return his ship and cargo and promised he would not take them to Guadeloupe "for fear of difficulties." Murray did not agree because the captain could not or would not furnish proof of ownership. Murray ordered the cargo, which was perishable, sold in Martinique. The proceeds were remitted to the bank of the United States, and the schooner was taken to St. Pierre. The matter would then be settled in court. Lieutenant Miles King was put aboard with orders to "pry" around the ship to learn all he could about her. Murray was suspicious. As he pointed out in his orders to Master's Mate John McFarline, who was to take the schooner to Philadelphia, "had she have been really Neutral property and in a Fair Trade, (she) would not have run for many hours directly to leeward and out of her tract from any Vessel . . ." The Danish government later demanded the return of *Charming Betsy.*

At Martinique, Murray found dispatches from Truxtun ordering him to Cape Francoise, Santo Domingo, where Toussaint L'Ouverture was leading the revolution with the aid of the United States. *Constellation* arrived at Cape Francoise on July 17, and found *Constitution* in harbor repairing some damage to her spars. Captain Talbot come out a week later and Murray relieved him in command of the squadron. In the same dispatch to Stoddert announcing his arrival and assumption of the command, Murray reported that he was having difficulty with *Constellation's* rudder. The rudder head had been split while the frigate was under Truxtun's command and he had made repairs in Hampton Roads. Murray was afraid it could never be made secure while at sea. He also reported that *Constellation* needed "an entire cleaning in the hold . . . which can not be well done without moving all her Ballast, which has never been done since she was first equipd & she is now getting full of Ratts & other Vermine which no common modes of cleansing can obviate."

On taking over his new command as Commodore, Murray's first task was to get in touch with Edward Stevens, the United States Consul in Santo Domingo, to establish contact with General Toussaint L'Ouverture and show the United States' friendliness to his cause. He also wanted Stevens to make arrangements to permit *Constellation* to moor in the Mole to repair her rudder. On July 31, Stevens finally came out to the frigate and "predicted (that) great political changes are likely to take place here." This was an understatement.

In his dispatch to Secretary Stoddert on July 31, Murray reported that *Norfolk* had just arrived from Cartagena, where the French privateers were operating in great numbers, "in a shattered and insecure state." He intended to take station off Cape St. Nicholas Mole in order to keep an eye out for *La Vengeance* which, he had been advised, was nearly ready for sea.

In closing his dispatch he included a paragraph that was an omen of another crisis which would come to a head in a few years:

I think Sir that we have no Enemy so much to be shunned in this quarter, as the British, for they blockade all the passages, & fair, or fowl, let few of our Vessels pass them, if they have Cargoes of Value, and send them to Jamaica, where the venality of the Admiralty Court gives no quarter, how long we are to bear with these agravations, I leave to wiser heads than mine to determine; but I confess I think we stand on very critical grounds with them; but as Admiral Parker is now gone home, let us hope for a favorable change of measures.

Of course, a favorable change of measures did not come about; instead, there was war twelve years later.

Although Great Britain had agreed to stop interfering with the United States' trade in the West Indies, her privateers in the Caribbean continued to seize American merchantmen on one pretext or another, and send them to Jamaica where the Admiralty Court, under Admiral Peter Parker, was notorious for the severity of its penalites.

On August 10, *Constellation* was back off Cape Francoise "after our unsuccessful excursion" and Captain Murray wrote Consul Stevens that the frigate's rudder was rapidly deteriorating. "I find it will now be absolutely necessary to take my ship into port to repair her rudder, unless anything of importance should transpire to make me try a little longer." To make his situation even worse, Murray reported that many of his crew were down with dysentery, several had died, and it would be most desirable to land about thirty of the invalids, as he did not think they could get well aboard ship. Stevens advised him that matters were coming to a head in Santo Domingo and that it was important to move a number of merchantmen in the harbor. Murray agreed to run the risk of losing his rudder and see the convoy through the passage, although he confessed that he could not give them much more than moral support if they were attacked. Arrangements were made to take forty-three patients ashore and leave them under the care of one of the "Doctrs Mates" until *Constellation* returned.

On August 21, while they were at sea, *Constellation* met *Trumbull,* Master Commandant David Jewett commanding, soon after she had captured the 8-gun privateer schooner *Vengeance,* and her passengers, whom Murray considered to be the worst band of cut-throats he had ever seen. They were apparently bound for Santo Domingo to fight against Toussaint L'Ouverture. Jewett was ordered to take *Vengeance* directly to Norfolk, advise the Naval Agent there of his arrival as soon as he came in, and let the Agent make arrangements for the disposition of the prisoners and schooner. Although denied some prisoners, L'Ouverture expressed his appreciation in a letter to the American captain before he sailed for home for "the marks of kindness and civility you have been pleased to show me."

Constellation's old adversary, *La Vengeance*, had, in the meantime, escaped "in a very lame condition" from Curacao, only to run into HMS *Seive*, a 44-gun vessel the British had captured from the French in 1798. *La Vengeance* was easily taken. Strange as it seems, some vessels actually served under British, French and American flags in their checkered and sometimes battered careers.

On August 28, Murray wrote Stoddert from Cape Francoise that he was in the port and had hoisted *Constellation's* damaged rudder aboard. He found it "in a very rotten, and crazy condition." Repairs took longer than expected because of the difficulty in getting timber of sufficient size in Santo Domingo and because the ship's carpenter had been among the casualties of the "flux." Murray finally had to "vamp it up with two pieces," but felt that it was a satisfactory job.

By September 11, *Constellation* was ready to sail for home. She had been duly relieved by *Congress* and had only enough provisions on board to see her there. Most of the sick in the hospital ashore were taken aboard, but many had to be left in charge of Surgeon's Mate Frederick Bernard. He was ordered to send them back by available transportation as soon as possible, as it was costing the United States $100 a month rent for the house they were occupying.

By September 18, *Constellation* was off Morro Castle, Havana, and Murray sent Lieutenant Ambrose Shirley ashore to contact the United States Consul to find out if any American ships wanted convoy, or if there were any moneys to be transported back to the States. As *Constellation* was running short of provisions, Captain Murray planned to stop in Havana for only two or three days, but the frigate's reception in port played havoc with his schedule.

On his return to the ship, Shirley informed his captain that the Cuban authorities wished him to enter the harbor. Salutes were exchanged with Morro Castle as *Constellation* passed the old fort. A letter from Havana, reprinted in the *New York Gazette and General Advertiser* describes the events that followed:

After the usual offer of services, which is uniformly practiced by the government, and especially by the Navy Department, towards American state ships, the barge of the *St. Pedro de Alcantra*, ship of the line, commanded by D. Dionna Galiano, went on board the *Constellation*, with a card, inviting Captain Murray, and his officers to an entertainment, to be given next day to the Ex-Vice-Roi of Mexico Don Joseph Mique de Asanza, at present here. Captain Murray on landing, went with the Consul to visit all the constituted authorities, by whom he was received with the most pointed marks of politeness, and every officer tendered him in person. —Agreeably to invitation Captain Murray and his officers went on board the *St. Pedro*, where two officers were stationed for the express purpose of waiting the arrival of the American commander, on which being announced, Captain Galiano came to the gangway to receive him, and seated him in the most distinguished part of the assembly.

The next day, Captain Galiano dined on board the *Constellation;* and the day following Admiral Aristinbil and Vice Admiral Nuenoz, waited on Captain Murray, who being apprised of it, hoisted all his colors elegantly dressed.—As soon as they were on deck, a salute of 15 guns was fired. They were very much pleased with the ship, and insisted that she was not a frigate, but a ship of the line. When they returned on shore, the yards were again manned, and three cheers given them by the crew. The circumstance of dressing the ship gave rise to some ill timed jealousy on the part of a French captain of a privateer, who supposed an affront was intended his nation because the French colours happened to be laced below the American and the English. It produced a very scurrilous letter to Captain Murray, which being known by the Governor he ordered the captain and lieutenants of the privateer to confinement. Upon the whole, these circumstances, the appearance of the ship, and the excellent discipline which is maintained on board has made impressions extremely favorable to the character of our rising navy.

All in all, *Constellation's* favored reception in Havana certainly would have had repercussions in European diplomatic circles, especially in Madrid and Paris, save for the signing of a treaty between the United States and France early the next year.

A party-weary vessel departed from Havana on September 23, with the northbound convoy. HMS *Thunderer* was met a short time later, but she made no effort to detain the convoy when Murray assured the British commander that the ships were under his protection. The convoy was dismissed at latitude 27° N. *Constellation* encountered a heavy gale off Cape Hatteras and was found to be leaking badly, but arrived in Delaware Bay without suffering any damage. *Constellation* then proceeded up the bay and anchored off New Castle, Delaware on October 10.

Secretary Stoddert was disappointed at Murray's choice of New Castle, and on receiving the report of his arrival wrote him that if *Constellation* needed repairs he was to proceed to New York. With so many ships already in Delaware Bay and the season so far advanced, the Secretary was afraid he might get caught in the freeze-up. On October 15, he sent Murray definite orders to go to New York, pay off his crew, and "have every arrangement made for putting the ship in proper order to receive another crew."

Once again the slowness of communications of the day interfered with the Secretary's plans, for by the time Murray had received his orders to go to New York, he had moved *Constellation* up to Marcus Hook and work on the frigate had already started. In his letter to Secretary Stoddert on October 18, Murray expressed his regret but pointed out that the orders he had received from Captain James Sever of *Congress* were that he was to go to New Castle. He felt that the cost of moving his ship again and the delay involved would be extraordinary and thought that they could get the work completed before winter came: ". . . her Bends are the worst Job, which are very much Worm eaten owing to the great fault in not coppering her high enough at first, for they have never been out of Water since she was first fitted out." His superior agreed with Murray but urged him to hurry the work along. He wanted *Constellation* back on station as soon as possible.

Meanwhile, a treaty had been negotiated between the representatives of the United States and the Republic of France, and was signed on September 30. No official word of this treaty had yet been received when Secretary Stoddert wrote his orders for *Constellation* to proceed to sea and "shape your course as your Judgement shall direct, to afford most protection to American Vessels bound from the E. Indies & Europe, to the U. States." The Secretary had received intelligence that "a ship of 24 guns, two or three brigs & a schooner from Cayenne, are cruising to intercept Vessels so bound." Eight to ten weeks after his departure from the States, Captain Murray was directed to call at the Guadeloupe station to learn of the situation with France; in the meantime, he was to capture any French vessels, as it was reasoned that their only purpose in being in the area would be to intercept American ships. If he learned, on good authority, from American ships that the Treaty had been signed, or if he found that French national ships were not capturing American vessels, "you will in that case not seek encounters with them—but you will not avoid encounters if sought on their part." If he found no orders from Stoddert when he called at St. Kitts, Murray was directed to consult with the Commanding Officer there and employ *Constellation* thereafter as the two of them thought best.

However, when *Constellation* sailed from New Castle on December 11, her destination was New York, to take on supplies not available at New Castle. She left before her medical officer and her lieutenant of marines had reported aboard, and she had to leave one of her surgeon's mates behind because of illness. At the last minute Murray discharged his sailing master, who had "never been worth his Salt," and wrote the Naval Agent in New York to engage another for the frigate. As usual, the purser was behind with his accounts but Murray assured Stoddert that they would be in shape by the time they were ready to leave New York. (The Navy had an ironclad rule that no purser could sail until his accounts ashore were settled.)

The text of the treaty between the United States and France had arrived in Washington and was transmitted to the Senate for ratification on December 15. Under these circumstances, Captain Murray found orders awaiting him on his arrival in New York directing him to remain there until he received further instructions.

With so many new officers aboard Murray drew up a new set of standing orders. The midshipmen were enjoined to pay more attention to their duties. He also reminded them promotion depended on the recommendations of the commanding officer. The commissioned officers were told that "the Quarter Deck (was) never to be left without a Commissioned Officer, if it can be avoided, all other regulations laid down for the Government of the Navy to be observed as usual."

With the treaty still under consideration by the Senate on December 30, Secretary Stoddert ordered *Constellation* to

96

sea to protect American commerce if the French were still operating against United States ships. She was to sail for St. Kitts with a convoy for the Windward Islands and deliver letters to Captains Barry and Truxtun; that mission accomplished she was to cruise around the West Indian islands providing convoy to American vessels for two months and then report to St. Kitts for further orders. Armed French vessels were to be treated "exactly as you find they treat American, Trading Vessels."

Constellation's pilot was dropped off Sandy Hook on January 9, after a delay in getting to sea caused by the wind dropping and ice in the Bay. Passing over the bar, *Constellation* touched bottom several times but her captain did not think she sustained any damage. On January 12, she ran into foul weather as her captain logged.

. . .we encountered a tremendous Gale of Wind from the South S West in Latt. 37.30, which continued with little intermission for 24 Hours, & come on in a very sudden manner, every effort was made to place the ship in as safe a situation as possible,—top gallant yards, & Masts down etc, but while scudding under a reeft fore sail. (the only sail we could set,) the Lee sheet gave way, & brought us by the Lee, the sea making a perfect breach over us, stove in all our ports, & in a few minutes we had near six feet of water in the Hold, the most of which entered our Hatchways before we could get them properly secured, in this situation, I was perswaided to cut away the Mizzen Mast & began to cut the Lee shrouds & stays & some of the weather ones, when we succeeded in getting aft the Lee fore Tack, & a preventer sheet, which payed her off before the wind, at that moment we ceased cutting away, & proceeded to get preventer Tackles upon the mast to save it, & get down the Gaff, but not till it gave a crack which gave us great alarm yet finally we secured it, & have it now in a safe state, still the pumps gained but little on the Water in the Hold, & we contemplated throwing overboard our spar Deck Guns but after great exertions, we brough the pumps to suck, in the course of which time, I was eighteen Hours on the Deck without rest, as were the greater part of the Crew, continually expecting to be obliged to cut away the masts the next day, we made sail under close reeft Main & Fore top sails, till by degrees we had a return of moderate weather, to put things again in Order, tho we had a good deal of Bread damaged . . . nothing but the strength of the ship saved us, our dander (sic) was eminent.

So Murray had nearly run *Constellation* aground and later tried to chop her mizzen down quite unnecessarily. Was he not so lucky as Truxtun, or was he not the seaman?

Then there was another near-tragedy on the run to the West Indies. During the night, when the frigate was in latitude 22° N, she passed a large ship which fired on her. *Constellation* returned the fire and then made the recognition signal for the night, which was answered in part. On hailing, it was found she was the 48-gun British frigate *Magnanime,* Neither ship sustained material damage, and, needless to say, both captains were red-faced over the unwanted encounter. Murray did learn from the British that the French were still attacking American ships.

On January 17, *Constellation* captured the 14-gun French lugger *Mars,* sailing from Guadeloupe with a crew of one hundred. On close examination of her papers, *Mars* was found to be under orders not to attack American vessels for the "war" was over. The lugger was returned to Captain Prosper Sergente and his crew. Murray was given an affidavit that nothing had been removed from her and that if hostilities "are yet pursued by France & the United States," Sergente would surrender his ship to American authorities. In return Murray gave the French captain a letter requesting other American vessels to let him pass and a letter to the agents of the French consuls in the Windward Islands at Port Liberty asking information about their attitudes.

On January 27, *Constellation* recaptured the American brig *Pride* and Lieutenant Robert Warren was put aboard to sail her to St. Kitts with instructions (if he met the *United States* or *President* on the way) to inform Captains Barry or Truxtun that Murray had dispatches for them. Murray had intended to sail for Basseterre and wait for the French reply to the letter he had sent with Captain Sergente, but at the last minute he changed his mind and proceeded directly to Port Liberty, where he arrived January 29.

Constellation's reception at Port Liberty was most cordial. The French general came aboard to welcome the American frigate. *Constellation* anchored under the guns of the fort, and Captain Murray and the general went ashore together to celebrate the peace. After two days of "feasting and bands of musick" Murray agreed to carry dispatches to the French agents on the outlying islands notifying them of the cessation of hostilities. In his report to Secretary Stoddert from Basseterre, Murray said that he intended to call at Porto Rico and then Havana to deliver his messages and then proceed to the Delaware where he hoped to arrive in March or April.

The month of February was spent in cruising among the Leeward Islands carrying the word that the Quasi-War was over and making calls at St. Thomas, Porto Rico, and Cape Francois. A course was then shaped for Havana, where *Constellation* found a convoy with which she sailed for Delaware Bay on March 2.

On his arrival at Havana, Captain Murray found *Constellation's* mizzenmast so weak that it would have to be hoisted out and "more securely fished." He estimated the job would delay him a week or ten days. He reported to Stoddert that "the English Privateers are playing the very Devil with our commerce, they want a little overhauling & I fear will amount to something serious in the end."

Now she was to go home from the wars. *Constellation's* record in the Quasi-War is one seldom equalled by a fighting ship: one frigate captured, one frigate defeated, three privateers captured, four privateers sunk, seventy merchant vessels recaptured, and the seizure of American ships greatly reduced. In Europe, the French at last began to realize the United States would fight anyone, even the greatest powers if necessary.

By the time *Constellation* came to anchor in Delaware Bay in the third week of March, 1801, Thomas Jefferson had been inaugurated as the third president of the United States and an administration dedicated to cutting governmental expenses, even at the cost of national security, was in power in Washington. In a last minute rush to retain some semblance of a Navy, the outgoing Federalist Congress had incorporated Secretary of the Navy Stoddert's recommendations in a Peace Establishment Act that was passed on March 3, and signed by President Adams before he turned the presidency over to his successor the following day.

One of the earliest photos of Constellation.

Annapolis, Md., 1879

This act authorized the President to retain thirteen frigates in the Peace Establishment and to dispose of all other vessels of the Navy. Seven of the retained frigates were to be laid up in ordinary while the remaining six were to be kept active, but manned by only two-thirds of their normal complement of seamen. All but nine captains, thirty-six lieutenants, and 150 midshipmen were to be discharged from the service, and those that remained on the list were to serve on half pay when not under orders for active duty. The thirteen frigates that were to constitute the United States Navy were: *United States,* 44 guns, *Constitution,* 44 guns, *President,* 44 guns, *Constellation,* 36 guns, *Chesapeake,* 36 guns, *Philadelphia,* 36 guns, *Congress,* 36 guns, *New York,* 36 guns, *Essex,* 32 guns, *Adams,* 28 guns, *Boston,* 28 guns, and *General Greene,* 28 guns.

That most unfortunate American policy pattern was in the process of being established. Again and again in our history, military and naval forces would be permitted to atrophy until the next emergency found us unprepared and frantically scrambling to get ready. At the time of the Peace Establishment, new difficulties with the Barbary States were brewing and relations with the British becoming more strained.

The nation's first Secretary of the Navy stayed on until his successor could be chosen, and did his best to prevent a complete breakdown in naval operations. On March 16, Stoddert wrote Murray that because of the uncertainty he was not to proceed farther up the bay than New Castle, and the frigate was accordingly anchored two miles below Fort Casimir. On March 21, Murray wrote a worried letter to Stoddert asking for a "hint" as to what was to be done with *Constellation* and himself; the Secretary replied that the crew of *Constellation* was to be paid off, although the year's enlistment of many had not expired, and only a caretaker's cadre left aboard. He offered no hint as to Murray's future.

On April 1, Secretary of War Henry Dearborn assumed the additional job of Acting Secretary of the Navy, and Secretary Stoddert retired, relieved that he did not have to select the nine captains to be retained on the active list. Before he left, however, he ordered Captain Murray to take *Constellation* up to Philadelphia for decommissioning. Acknowledging this order, Murray pointed out that he had no instructions about who, among the officers, was to be retained and that he supposed that the only things to be removed from the frigate would be the sails, powder, and provisions "which are liable to Waste and damage on board." *Constellation* arrived in Philadelphia on April 2, 1801.

On April 11, Secretary Dearborn wrote Murray that as *Constellation* was to be laid up, no money was to be expended on anything but upkeep repairs, and that the request for a new cable and the badly needed mizzenment was denied; he also indicated that all the ships scheduled to be laid up were to be taken to Washington. But before this disheartening news was received, a catastrophe occurred that resulted in a complete change of plans for the frigate.

On Friday night, April 6, a stiff northwest wind caused *Constellation* to drag one of her anchors and go aground in the Delaware River. In his preliminary report of the accident, Captain Murray wrote that the frigate had grounded "at nearly high Water upon a hard Rock and sand bottom but little known to the best Pilots in this River & was only dangerous to Ships of our great draft of Water, but before timely assistance could be afforded, the Tide Ebb'd so fast she lay down almost on her Beem ends, every effort was made to prevent the mischief that hath ensued, but to no purpose she soon filled with Water, with all her guns & stores on board the Powder & Sails excepted we are now making every exertion in our power to get her upon an even keel so that we may be enabled to get out her guns etc etc."

Murray's "accident proneness" had recurred once again. Meanwhile, many of *Constellation's* veteran midshipmen, Tilghman, Gardner, Stewart, Mason, Nicholson, and Truxtun's son Thomas, were detached and ordered to the ill-fated frigate *Philadephia.* Tom, only seventeen, would shortly resign his commission and be lost at sea only a year later, while on his first merchant voyage.

The next three weeks were spent getting *Constellation* afloat. On April 26, Captain Murray reported that he expected to have the job finished in "a day or two" and that the cost would "not much exceed $5000." He then advised Secretary Dearborn that "the *Constellation* is of the greatest draft of Water of any Ship in the U.S. service & cannot be brought to a less draft than 19 or 20 feet, with all her guns & stores out her common draft is 22.6 Inches." If he had known that the Department wanted her taken to Washington, he wrote, it could have been done at very little expense as at least two-thirds of the crew still had time to serve on their enlistments. As things now stood it would be a very expensive movement as "every Article must be got out & dryed and a great part of her Riggin is very much injured or destroyed from the situation in which she lay when we strip'd her of her Tackling." He advised that the damaged cordage and stores be sold in Philadelphia.

In closing this report to Secretary Dearborn, Murray wrote a more detailed account of the accident and endeavored to clear himself of any blame. Despite the excuses and mitigation, Murray had anchored in an unfavorable and dangerous anchorage, his anchor had not bit, and he did not take soundings around his scope. It was poor seamanship that cause the grounding.

On May 3, *Constellation* was again afloat and pumped dry. Murray planned to move her to a wharf next day and discharge everything on board "to cleanse her of the Mud and filth collected since the misfortune." He requested officers to replace those who had been detached (he had one lieutenant, the Sailing Master, and the Gunner on board) if he was to take the frigate to Washington. Also, he wanted a crew of at least two hundred men. *Constellation,* he reported, drew 20 feet aft and 19.4 feet forward "stripped as she is of everything but her Ballast." Secretary Dearborn wanted all the soaked and useless gear surveyed and sold at auction.

Captain Murry, still in the dark as to whether he would be retained on the active list, advised Dearborn that it would be cheaper to repair *Constellation* and keep her in Philadelphia, "where she lays at a good snug Wharf at the expense of only $3 pr day Wharfage," than to move her to Washington. His letter continued:

. . . . she now lays stripped of everything but her lower Masts, and her Riggin from urgent necessity promiscuously scattered about without a Tally or dissignation and a good deal of it cut . . . . then let us take into consideration the expence of equipment, for the removal of so heavy a Ship will require at least 200 Men even for so short a trip . . . . after all, if ever her services are required this expence must be incurr'd, besides the repairs she requires cannot be procured at Washington again if she is to be laid up in her present state.

Secretary Dearborn and President Jefferson decided to have the ship repaired in Philadelphia and "put on the Peace Establishment as soon as we can provide a proper sailing Master." Lieutenant Brooke was ordered to stay on board, and Captain Murray was expected to superintend the repairs.

Murray started the repairs and was having the rotten planks removed when he was called to Washington, where he was notified that he was not to be retained on the active list. A second survey of *Constellation* was ordered. Murray was sorely disappointed. On July 7, he wrote to Dearborn that they were still awaiting the results of the second survey, and after detailing his past service in the Navy, asked rather plaintively why he had been passed over. If he was to superintend *Constellation's* repairs, he wanted to have his status clarified. On September 30, Robert Smith, who had become the new Secretary of the Navy, advised him that *Constellation* was to "be put in complete order for Service" and requested his opinion on the criticism that *Constellation* was over-masted.

Murray replied that *Constellation* was progressing well, and he reported, "when finished will be a noble ship & do credit to any nation." Furthermore, he said, he had made arrangements to mount 44 guns, if Secretary Smith thought proper, "as she is much larger & better able to carry them than either the *Philadelphia* or *Chesapeake*."

It was not a good idea. Truxtun had always felt that *Constellation*'s draft was too great as it was and that she had also been considered too sluggish. That was the reason the 24's originally in her main battery had been replaced with 18-pounders. Smith wanted more information. Did Murray think she was sufficiently stiff when he sailed her? Did he think that the contemplated reduction in the size of her spars would keep her "duly poised" if the additional guns were put aboard? Would not such an alteration sink her so deeply in the water and, by increasing the resistance, interfere with her sailing and make her carry her guns too low? "As there are no Mathematical Rules for ascertaining the most eligible proportions to be observed in Naval Architecture, the defect must be supplied by observation & experience," Smith replied. "I must wait therefore, for your answer before I can take order on the subject of Alteration, you have suggested."

Replying to the Secretary's letter, Captain Murray wrote:

From the time I took Command of *Constellation* till her arrival here I have at various times encountered heavy gales of wind, & found her sufficiently stiff but like all sharp built ships will lay over upon a press of sail till she gets to her bearings after which she will bear the press as long as any ship whatever.

I am now confident that the reduction we have made of the spars as well as her upper works will enable me to leave out 30 Tons of Ballast, which will reduce her draft of water & that she will sail infinitely faster than ever I have likewise altered her masts & further, as it was found necessary to pull down most of the store Rooms, for the Carpenters to work I have made such large reductions to some & thrown superfluous ones into the Bread & Spirit Rooms before too small that she will now carry one months stores more than ever it did & this placed in the hold of the ship, to counterpoise the reduction of the Ballast, whereas previously great weight of stores were carried up in her birth Deck she had always a superfluous quantity of Lumber which I shall now dispense with . . .

With regard to the addition of guns I have ever since I commanded her mounted 40 guns those I contemplate mounting are light 24 lb carronades for the Qr Deck similar to what she now has a pair of them are now in the Navy Yard ready fitted so that little or no expence will be incurr'd nor will I ever wish to have more than 320 Men her usual crew peace or War for 44 guns.

I have no doubt but the most competent judges will now pronounce her to be of the most compleat & convenient ships in the service & will be ready when required.

Secretary Smith agreed to Murray's proposal that *Constellation* be converted to a 44-gun vessel and asked when she would be ready for sea, as he wanted her on active service early the next year. Murray announced optimistically that she could sail on November 14.

The carpentry was finished on December 1, and Murray was sure he would sail in three weeks. He thought his vessel was now better than she was "at her first outfit, being nearly rebuilt from the Water edge upwards, with great improvements, & her timbers well salted to prevent a future rot." Perhaps his recollection of the prior grounding led Murray to suggest waiting until the ice broke in February or March, before attempting to cross the bar at Fort Mifflin, where the depth was only twenty feet at high water. This, it will be recalled, was *Constellation's* draft without her guns or water aboard.

Constellation's old skipper, in the meantime, was having his troubles. Truxtun made one cruise in *President,* as commodore of a powerful squadron, but the Quasi-War with France was sputtering to a halt and he saw little action. Commodore Barry relieved Truxtun on station in January, 1801. Returning home, the commodore learned that Thomas Jefferson was the new president and the Anti-Federalists, so opposed to expenditures for military and naval purposes, were in power. There was no chance to be admiral now; it would be lucky if the Navy itself survived.

Without the French to fight, Truxtun turned his personal guns on the Government and revived the Talbot-senority controversy. On April 2, 1801, Commodore Truxtun received orders from the Navy Department to take command of the Mediterranean Squadron. He refused to go. The squadron was going only to "show the flag," and the fighting sailor wanted to "bang" the pirates, not to play games with them. The Secretary said no fighting, and Truxtun was relieved by Captain Richard Dale.

The Government remained patient. In January, 1802, he again received orders to the Mediterranean once more, this time to relieve Dale with a second squadron. He could not refuse.

By this time, Jefferson had appointed Robert Smith of Maryland permanent Secretary of the Navy. A Baltimore man, Robert Smith had known and disliked Truxtun for years. The feeling was mutual. Now Truxtun began to complain again. Some of his gripes were legitimate; at other times he played prima donna. His flagship *Chesapeake* was too small, and he wanted to shift his flag to *Constellation* when he reached the Mediterranean. *Chesapeake* was in a disgracefully neglected condition when he reported on board her at the Norfolk Navy Yard. She was manned by one officer and a skeleton crew. Truxtun had been promised a flag captain for *Chesapeake,* so that he would not have to be both commodore of the squadron and skipper of the ship. It was a point of pride for him, like so many other things. After all, Dale had a flag captain with him on station now. Despite the promises, neither a captain nor an adequate crew were forthcoming from Smith, and it seemed to Truxtun, perhaps correctly, that the squeeze was on. Characteristically and expectedly, Truxtun resigned his commission in the Navy. It may have been a ploy on his part, thinking that Smith would not dare to let him go. He was sadly mistaken. The resignation was immediately accepted.

So Truxtun was on the beach for good. He wrote letter after letter complaining of the treatment he had received, But he was not to lead the Navy against the Barbary States even though Commodores Dale and Richard V. Morris would blunder badly in the first crack at the pirates, neither having Truxtun's intrepidity or his sheer aggressiveness. Truxtun would walk the beach during the War of 1812, shaking his head, never quite understanding, along with so many others, why we were fighting the British instead of Napoleon. Thus, the Father of the Navy passed slowly and quietly into history.

But new events were in the making. The French had been contained and defeated in all major actions and the Navy's attention was turning to the Barbary Coast. *Constellation* was destined for Mediterranean duty.

War With The Barbary States

During the five years that followed the signing in 1795 of a treaty of peace between Algiers and the United States, the Barbary States appeared content to collect their annual payments of tribute money and supplies. They permitted American merchantmen to trade in the Mediterranean without molestation by their corsairs, who were occupying themselves with the ships of other nationalities. However, as George Washington had predicted in 1796, the lull was only temporary. In the early months of 1800, the Bashaw of Tripoli, Yusaf Karamanli, began to intimate that he was dissatisfied with this treaty. United States merchantmen were doing business at Mediterranean ports to the sum of $8,800,000 in 1799, and $11,900,000 in 1800, and the Bashaw wanted a "bigger cut."

Summoning United States Counsul James Leander Cathcart to the palace, he stated the reasons for his dissatisfaction bluntly: Tunis and Algiers were getting more attention than Tripoli, in spite of the fact that his country was acknowledged superior to the other two. The United States had made the Dey of Algiers a present of the frigate *Crescent*—now he wanted one, too—and the Sahibtappa at Tunis had received many presents from the United States in addition to forty thousand dollars in cash; he (the Bashaw) had gotten little more although he was much more powerful. The Bashaw followed up this interview with a letter to President Adams in which he reiterated his demands and threatened to declare war. The Bashaw was displeased with the American reply, and on May 14, 1801 he ordered the flag pole in front of the United States Consulate cut down and formally declared war.

Meanwhile, the Bey of Tunis raised the price of peace with his country since Sweden, Denmark, Spain, and Sicily had agreed earlier to increase their tribute payments. The American Consul was told that some of the stores sent to the Bey from the United States were unsatisfactory and that other articles had not been forwarded according to the agreement of 1795. On April 15, 1801, the Bey addressed a letter to President Jefferson renewing his request for forty 24-pounder guns, and two months later he told the Consul that unless he was given ten thousand stands of arms without delay, he would declare war.

To make matters still worse, the United States was in arrears in its payments to Algiers, and the Dey was very irritated. Richard O'Brien, the American Consul at Algiers, could not conceal his apprehension in a letter to the U.S. Minister at Lisbon:

> Even at this moment, I shudder for fear of our valuable vessels and citizens in this sea—so much in arrears—no funds, no corsairs, and threatened by all the dogs of prey. Algiers, a pirate state, wants employment for the refractory and for their corsairs. The troubles of the Baltic will scare the Swedes and Danes into port, and we in arrears—no *oil* in our lamps, no anchors and cables, no corsairs in this sea: we will be the victims.

Although the news that Tripoli had declared war on the United States had not yet reached Washington, the government was aware of the hostility of the Barbary States and the unprotected condition of American vessels in the Mediterranean. Hoping that a show of force off the North African ports might prevent their rulers from committing overt acts, a "squadron of observation"—consisting of the frigates *President, Philadelphia,* and *Essex* and the schooner *Enterprize*—under the command of Commodore Richard Dale was ordered to sail for Gibraltor. He was to carry tribute payments due Algiers and Tripoli.

As the United States government was uncertain of the actual state of affairs in the Mediterranean, Commodore Dale was ordered to call at Algiers, Tunis and Tripoli, and if war had not already been declared by the individual states, to deliver the payments. If any or all of the Barbary States had declared war on the United States, he was told to distribute his forces to protect American commerce.

On his arrival at Gibraltar, Dale found that Tripoli had declared war, but that Tunis and Algiers were still nominally at peace with his country. He visited the Dey of Algiers and the Bey of Tunis and mollified their grievances by delivery of thirty thousand dollars in gold. Proceeding to Tripoli, Commodore Dale set up a blockade with *President* and *Philadelphia.* He ordered *Essex* and *Enterprize* to cruise between Tripoli and Tunis to intercept any vessels captured by the Tripolitans.

Constellation all the while had been lying idle in Delaware Bay, ready to sail wherever the Secretary of the Navy might see fit to send her.

As the enlistments of the crews of Commodore Dale's squadron would expire in the spring, arrangements had to be made for their relief. On January 10, 1982, *Constellation* was ordered to prepare for sea. Captain Alexander Murray was still in command. *Constellation* would join Commodore R.V. Morris' squadron, relieving Dale at the blockade of Tripoli.

The month of February and the first week of March were filled with disappointments and frustrations for the men aboard *Constellation.* On February 2, Captain Murray wrote Secretary Smith that seamen in Philadelphia were holding out for higher wages and were threatening those who had enlisted. As he was anxious to get enough of a crew aboard to take the frigate down to New Castle, where he could load his guns and stores, he was considering sending some of his officers to New York to set up a recruiting rendezvous. At the same time, Murray made plans to take advantage of the spring tide of the February full moon to float *Constellation* over the bar below Fort Mifflin; but, a strong northwest wind interfered, and soundings revealed a mere nineteen feet of water, while the frigate drew twenty feet. It was not until

February 26, that Murray was able to get his ship over the bar. At Chester, he had to work day and night to get the stores aboard.

On March 7, *Constellation* was still at New Castle where foul weather had prevented loading the stores. The day before, a very heavy gale had parted their best bower cable, and the frigate was only saved from further accident by the sheet anchor. To cap all their misfortunes, almost fifty men were sick and two had died. Before she got out of the bay, *Constellation* lost another anchor.

Congress, on February 6, 1802, authorized United States armed vessels "to subdue, seize and make prize of all vessels, foods & effects belonging to the Bey of Tripoli or his subjects." Captain Murray received a copy of the instructions for the guidance of the captains of the various ships, and Commodore Dale was directed to blockade Tripolitan ports and provide escorts for American merchantmen in the Mediterranean.

At last, *Constellation* sailed from New Castle on March 13, 1802, with Gibraltar as her next port of call. *Constellation* was passing north of the Canary Islands and enjoying good weather. On April 20, a schooner four days out from Gibraltar was met and her captain reported that he reckoned his longitude as 17°W, while Murray believed they were at 14°48′W. This discrepancy bothered Captain Murray until he recalled that he was allowing only 45′ for a mile whereas he should have used 48′, "which would have made me nearly right."

The frigate made a landfall on April 30 at Malaga, and Murray wrote that they had been frustrated for the previous four weeks by a head easterly wind that had occasionally reached gale strength. Near Gibraltar the wind shifted to the west and Murray was fearful of trusting his ship as she still had only one anchor. The 80-gun HMS *Caesar* was met while he was trying to make up his mind, and when he learned that none of the United States squadron was at Gibraltar, he decided to run to Malaga and advise the United States Consul of his arrival. He then planned to sail to Carthagena to try to get anchors and cables, or to Toulon if his first call was unsuccessful. As he expected to fall in with the United States squadron off Tripoli, he would then shape a course for that area. Fortunately, *Philadelphia* and *Essex* were lying in the Malaga Roads, and the former was able to give *Constellation* a bower anchor in return for some stores.

On May 4, *Constellation* again got underway with *Philadelphia* and *Essex* in company and on the following day the three frigates anchored at Gibraltar. The British admiral, Lord Keith, was saluted with fifteen guns; he returned with thirteen.

Constellation received a cordial welcome at Gibraltar and Captain Murray lost no time in inquiring about the availability of another anchor and new cable. The captains of the British men-of-war at the base visited the frigate, and Captain Murray and his officers were invited to dine on the flagship *Foudroyant.* On May 10, the officers and men of the three American frigates were treated to a traditional show of pomp and circumstance by the Royal Navy when the Duke of Kent, Governor of Gibraltar, and a son of King George III, arrived in the 50-gun *Isis,* with the royal standard flying at the main.

The three frigates departed Gibraltar next morning. *Essex* and the ill-fated *Philadelphia* were homeward bound, and *Constellation* headed for Tripoli. By May 15, *Constellation* was about three leagues off Cape Alberto, when the wind dropped and a strong inshore current forced Murray to lower the boats and tow the frigate for an hour and a half until a breeze gave her steerageway. Two days later she reached Algiers, where the United States Consul, Richard O'Brien, came aboard with the ominous news that Algeria had twelve warships at sea and had captured a 46-gun Portugese frigate.

May 28th found her off Tunis, and Murray sent a boat ashore to contact Consul William Eaton. At the Captain's request Eaton came aboard the next day, remained overnight, and arranged to have *Constellation* freshly provisioned with fruits and vegetables. A supply of London-made arms that *Constellation* had picked up at Gibraltar was presented—on behalf of the United States—to the Bey of Tunis. The Bey was overjoyed, but demanded, as a further token of American goodwill, a corvette or brig of war such as Algiers had received.

Constellation left Tunis early on the morning of June 4, and four days later spoke the flagship and frigate of a Swedish squadron in company with the *Boston*. It was decided, as the Swedes were also at war with Tripoli, that the frigates would proceed to Tripoli, together. This they did, but scarcely had Captain Murray arrived in Tripolitan waters, when on June 11, he notified Captain McNeill of *Boston* that *Constellation's* water was getting low and that he would have to run over to Malta or Syracuse to fill his casks. *Boston* was ordered to continue the blockade.

Constellation arrived in the Bay of Saragosa on June 14, and the following week was spent in filling the water casks, giving the crew a turn on shore, and visiting ancient Syracuse. Underway again at 5 A.M., June 23, the frigate returned to Tripoli and cruised back and forth in front of the city close enough to the shore that the minarets were visible from her decks. *Boston* was detached on the 27th to proceed to Malta for stores, and *Constellation* continued the blockade with the two Swedish frigates. No contacts were made with the enemy as the days passed, and there was still no word of the arrival of *Chesapeake* or *Adams* in the Mediterranean.

On July 13, a neutral brig bound from Alexandria to Leghorn was chased, boarded and released. A few hours after discharging the brig, the Swedish frigate *Thetis* hove in sight. She was found to be carrying a flag of truce from Tripoli, and Captain Murray granted permission for a vessel flying the Ottoman flag and carrying Greek passengers to pass through the blockade.

At 4 A.M. on the morning of July 20, the lookout sighted a sail standing out from the city, and three hours later *Constellation* overtook a brig to which permission to pass had been given. She then chased another sail which she was unable to bring to before nightfall. *Thetis* was met and brought word of the capture of the American merchant brig *Franklin*.

Constellation had her first brush with the enemy two days later when several small sail were sighted. An hour into the chase, she was close enough to identify them as nine Tripolitan gun boats, and one of them opened fire on her. *Constellation* replied with her bow guns and bore away to give them her port broadside. A few minutes later the leadsman reported bottom at twelve fathoms and Captain Murray realized that he was being decoyed onto a reef. Orders were immediately given to wear ship, and as the frigates came about, the starboard guns were fired. *Constellation's* round shot began to find their mark. Fires broke out in the harassed gunboats. On the beach, the Tripolitan cavalry was drawn up six thousand strong. They opened fire with small arms—as if their musket balls could reach the frigate. Suddenly, several 18-pound shots cometed to the beach and landed among them, and they dispersed in a wild panic.

As *Constellation* bore away, the gunboats and forts opened fire but failed to score a hit. *Constellation's* only casualty was her spritsail yard which was damaged by a ball from one of her own 12-pounders. The engagement cost *Constellation* 370 pounds of powder, sixty round shot, twenty-two grape and twenty-one canister. But Captain Murray was later informed that her fire had killed the Bashaw's favorite general, who was standing on the beach only a few feet from the Bashaw himself, that eleven of their wounded had died, and that two gunboats had been destroyed.

On July 30, Murray wrote a report of the action to the Secretary of the Navy and advised him of the desirability of having on the blockade smaller vessels that could get in closer to the shore and be propelled by oars if necessary. He pointed out that the Tripolitans used small galleys, indistinguishable from the coastal craft, and were able to slip through the blockade under cover of darkness. If pursued, they took refuge in waters too shallow for the frigates to venture. Lack of small, light draft vessels would plague all the American commanders in the Mediterrean, he predicted. Murray said he had not yet had word of the arrival of the other ships of the squadron at Gibraltar. *Boston* had gone to Malta for supplies on June 26, and was long overdue, and the two Swedish frigates that had been on the station had departed to replenish their stores and were not expected back

before the middle of August. *Constellation* was maintaining
the blockade alone, and as he had supplied *Philadelphia* with
some of his stores, his own provisions were running low and
he would have to leave in ten days for more.

Early in the morning on August 1, the lookout sighted
three ships becalmed to the northward, and as soon as a
breeze came up *Constellation* gave chase. They were three
Danish men-of-war bound for Tripoli with Denmark's tribute
money. Murray must have been confounded by the sight of
three warships delivering tribute to a pirate. Small wonder
the corsairs had little respect for Europeans! They informed
Murray that Morocco also had declared war on the United
States and Sweden, and that two American frigates had arrived at Gibraltar.

The next two weeks passed peacefully, but Eaton, the
American Consul at Tunis, wanted more aggressive action.
Reporting to the Secretary of State on August 8, he complained that none of the commanders of the United States
squadron had communicated with him since *Constellation*
called on June 3. "Government," he wrote, "may as well send
out *quaker meeting-houses* to float about this sea as frigates
with Murrays in command. The friendly salutes he may
receive and return at Gibraltar produce nothing at Tripoli.
Have we but one Truxton [sic] and one Sterret [sic] in the
United States?"

On August 14, *Constellation* was fifty miles south of Malta.
Two days later, she entered the harbor at Valetta, and the
United States Consul came aboard with the intelligence he
had been able to gather. The following week was taken up
with watering, caulking, and loading fresh provisions.

When Commodore Richard V. Morris arrived in the
Mediterranean, Captain Murray relinquished his respon-
sibilities of senior officer afloat and gave the commodore his
estimate of the situation. Commodore Dale had accomplished
little; Morris would do less. He was an amiable older man and
a good seaman, but quite unequal to the task of a commodore.
For his entire year of command, Tripoli would remained
unblockaded and only one enemy warship would be taken.
Morris would go home in disgrace, be found guilty of in-

competency by a court of inquiry, and dismissed from the Navy.

By September 1, Murray decided that the blockade was useless and notified Consul Eaton that he would head for Naples and Leghorn, where he would pick up a convoy for Gibraltar before returning to Tunis. *Constellation* departed from Tunisian waters on September 10, called at Palermo and then made for Naples. It required four days to make the passage against head winds. Arriving in the Bay of Naples on September 17, Murray found a Spanish squadron and a British frigate already at anchor and he exchanged a fifteen gun salute with the Spanish admiral. On arriving, Captain Murray wrote to the Secretary of the Navy describing the difficulties of apprehending enemy vessels on the Barbary Coast.

Constellation's rudder pintle was repaired and shipped, and on September 26, she got underway with a convoy of a brig and a schooner. A week later they anchored in the road at Leghorn, and settled down to await the arrival of Commodore Morris in *Chesapeake*. He appeared finally on October 12, with *Enterprize* and a convoy.

When *Constellation's* rudder was unshipped at Naples to repair the broken pintle, it was found that the upper pintle was weak. It was not replaced at the time, as Murray thought they could get along with ordinary sailing although it would be unsafe to risk her "on an enemies coast, in any season; much less in this." On October 17, the frigate sailed from Leghorn with two American merchantmen, *Ann* and *Eliza*, but difficulties with the rudder forced her to put into Toulon two days later. After anchoring bow and stern, salutes were exchanged with the French admiral, the rudder unshipped, and the launch sent ashore to begin filling the water casks.

Constellation's rudder was promptly repaired in the French navy yard without charge, but Captain Murray objected when the customs people demanded the brig and schooner pay tonage money (port charges). If this practice of charging convoyed vessels every time they called at a port was continued, the tax would soon become so heavy that they would risk proceeding without convoy.

On October 23, *Constellation* again got underway for Gibraltar with *Ann* and *Eliza* under convoy. But misfortune again dogged the frigate; foul weather was encountered, the foremast and fore yard were sprung, and the bread stores ran out. Not until November 19, did they make Malaga Roads, and a boat was sent ashore to request permission to anchor in the mole. A pilot was taken aboard, *Constellation* was towed into the harbor, and the frigate let go her anchor abreast the mole head with lines running ashore. Preparations were immediately started to get the foremast out, which involved unbending the stay sail and all head sails, taking in the flying jib boom and top gallant masts, unreaving all the running rigging forward, lowering the fore and foretopsail yards and the foretopmast to the deck, and removing the foretop, and main yard, and rigging shears. Fortunately *John Adams* came in soon after the work started and was able to provide *Constellation* with stores. Two days later *Enterprize* arrived.

As *Constellation* had left a spare yard in Gibraltar, and plenty of stores were available there, Captain Murray ordered Captain Rodgers and *John Adams* to the Rock to pick up the yard and some provisions before joining Commodore Morris. *Enterprize* was ordered to join the commodore in Malta.

The foremast was taken ashore for repair and the crew were employed in overhauling the rigging, but colds plagued the men and by the end of November nearly one hundred were on the sick list. The spar was in such bad condition that the carpenters had to shape a new one.

John Adams returned on December 10, with *Constellation's* order for home, and the repairs were speeded up. Captain Murray lost no time in transmitting Secretary Smith's letter to Commodore Morris, advising him that he was preparing to leave Malaga.

Underway again, the convoy arrived at Gibraltar on December 18, where *Adams* was keeping an eye on the Tripolitan *Meshouda. Adams* was ordered to run over to Tangier to advise the United States Consul that *Constellation* intended to call there on her way home to pick up his dispatches and any intelligence he might have regarding Morocco's posture toward the United States.

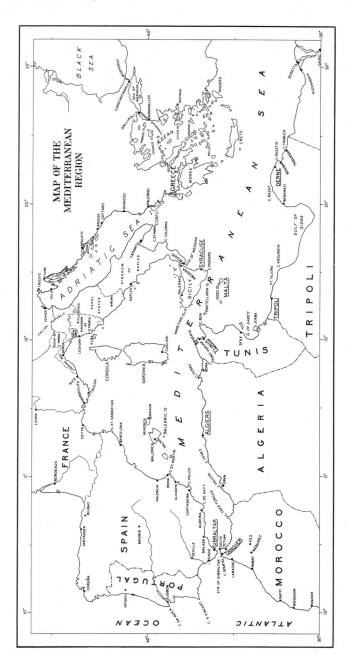

MAP OF THE MEDITERRANEAN REGION

Constellation was delayed a full month at Gibraltar as a result of bad weather; the wind had blown steadily from the west and had reached gale strength at least once every forty-eight hours. It was not until January 26, that a shift of wind to the east permitted *Constellation* to get out of the bay. Moderate and pleasant weather favored the frigate once she was in the Atlantic Ocean, and by February 6, she was south of the Canary Islands and not far from Cape Blanco. Captain Murray was again having trouble with his navigation, as his observed latitude did not agree with his dead reckoning calculations.

The weather was good, an occasional ship was met, and by March 10 *Constellation* made landfall. By evening she was abreast Cape Henry Light and the anchor was let go at the lower end of the Horseshoe with the light bearing "S.E.½". At seven o'clock next morning she got underway again and began to beat up the Bay. On March 12, the pilot was taken aboard and the frigate headed for the mouth of the Potomac River.

On his arrival in Chesapeake Bay, Captain Murray noted that the passage from Gibraltar to Cape Henry had taken thirty-nine days, of which ten had been spent "beating about" in the Gulf Stream in "dreadful tempestious, Weather, and head Winds so that we could scarcely carry any canvas to it," (although, oddly, the extracts from his journal indicate good weather all the way). Having forgotten to sign and date this report to Secretary Smith from Cape Henry, Murray wrote agin on March 12, after he had entered the Potomac, and reported that the pilot had advised him not to proceed farther up the river until he had lightened ship.

Disregarding this advice, Murray thought he could run up to the Shoals if the wind and tide were right, for otherwise he would have to get boats to take his guns ashore. *Constellation* got as far as Greenleaf Point (on the outskirts of Washington at the entrance to the Tidal Basin) where on March 15, she went aground. The cruise to Barbary ended with *Constellation* stuck fast. Fortunately, she soon floated off, and orders came to lay up in ordinary.

Meanwhile, Captain Edward Preble was ordered to relieve

Commodore Morris in command of the Mediterranean
Squadron. Preble was a New Englander who had distinguished himself as a privateersman in the Revolution. After
the war, he had entered the merchant service, becoming a
captain at the age of twenty-three. During the Quasi-War
with France, he had been commissioned as a lieutenant in the
Navy and served on *Constitution.* He was a taciturn, lonely
man, but had a keen analytical mind. He continued the tradition begun by Truxtun and *Constellation,* and he trained and
gave his nation a generation of magnificent naval officers,
who still called themselves "Preble's Boys" long after he had
gone.

Commodore Preble sailed for the Mediterranean in August,
1803. When he arrived at Gibraltar he found that *Philadelphia,* under William Bainbridge, had caught a Moroccan
warship in the act of seizing an American brig. Bainbridge
was waiting for Preble. The attack on the brig was an act of
war. What would the new Commodore do?

There was little time for conjecture. Preble immediately
moved the entire squadron and the captured ship to Tangier.
There, he cowed the Sultan into repudiating the actions of his
commander and renewing the treaty terms with the United
States. This was counted as a victory, for the treaty was not
altered. Preble had accomplished more in a few weeks than
his predecessors had in two years.

The Commodore now made a tactical error. He planned a
close blockade of Tripoli, the declared enemy of the United
States, and he ordered Captain Bainbridge to proceed in
Philadelphia with the 12-gun schooner *Vixen* as escort. Preble would follow with the squadron shortly. He had business
to complete in Tangier, and he was anxious to commence the
blockade.

But, off Tripoli Bainbridge met with disaster. Pursuing a
shallow draft Tripolitan, he ran *Philadelphia* onto an un-
charted reef. After a brief engagement he surrendered her to
the jubilant Tripolitans, who were able to refloat the vessel
after a gale loosed her. Now the enemy had one of his two
frigates, and Preble also had to worry about the captured
crew. Bringing up his squadron as soon as he learned the

news, Preble devised a plan to destroy *Philadelphia* and thus deprive the enemy of her use. The spirited Lieutenant Stephen Decatur, skipper of *Enterprize*, volunteered to take *Intrepid*—formerly *Mestico*, a captured, blockade-running ketch—under the enemy guns and destroy the captured frigate. On the night of February 7, 1804, Decatur and eighty-four volunteers from *Enterprize* sailed *Intrepid*, disguised as a supply vessel from Malta, into the harbor. There were two hundred enemy guns in position, but the Americans boarded *Philadelphia*, swept more than two hundred Tripolitans from the vessel in hand-to-hand combat, hauled their explosives on board, fired the ship, and shoved off with clockwork precision. They had just abandoned *Philadelphia* when she blew sky high. *Intrepid* danced out of Tripoli to the accompaniment of the bass notes of booming cannon.

Decatur was promoted to captain, and Preble continued to lead the offensive. He succeeded in persuading the authorities at Naples to lend him six gunboats and two mortar craft, and he enlisted ninety-six Neopolitan gunners, who served the American cause with distinction. These shallow draft vessels were badly needed for close inshore blockading.

The blockade was succeeding and the Bashaw was slowly being starved and pounded into submission, when Preble learned that a new squadron was on the way from the United States, and he was to be superseded in command of the squadron. The new commander, Captain Samuel Barron, was senior to Preble and command of the squadron had to be his.

When news of the capture of *Phildelphia* reached Washington in the latter part of March 1804, Congress at last appropriated one million dollars to authorize the recommissioning of enough ships to put an end to the Wars with the Barbary States. Accordingly, *President, Congress,* and *Essex,* were ordered back in service. With *John Adams,* these frigates were to augment the Mediterranean Squadron then operating under Preble. It was hoped that by May, the ships would be ready to sail with *John Adams. Constellation* was heading back to Barbary, now under Captain Hugh G. Campbell, former skipper of *Adams.*

The new reinforcements increased the United States squadron in the Mediterranean considerably: frigates *President, Congress, Constitution, Essex, Constellation;* brigs *Siren* and *Argus;* schooners *Vixen, Nautilus,* and *Enterprize.* The frigate *John Adams* acted as store ship.

Constellation, President, Essex, and *Congress* left Hampton Roads on July 3. A landfall was made on the island of Madeira on the 28th; they arrived at Gibraltar on August 12.

The frigates went on to Malta for water. *President* and *Constellation* followed the next day and joined Preble off Tripoli on September 10, while *Essex* and *Congress* went to Morocco to oversee the Sultan, who had been "angry" because Preble refused to permit two Moroccan ships loaded with wheat to enter Tripoli. The command of the Mediterranean Squadron was turned over to Captain Barron with the usual formalities, but Preble in *Constitution* remained.

President, Constellation, Constitution, and *Argus* remained off Tripoli for three more weeks, in the forlorn hope that the weather would permit them to attack the city, but then sailed for Malta and Syracuse. After a short leave period *Constellation* departed Malta for Tripoli in the company of *President, John Adams,* and *Siren.* Foul weather with gale winds and heavy squalls caused *Constellation* to lose all her head rails, and Captain Campbell reported she was "rendered very leaky in all her upper works particularly about the Bows, in so much that for some time we had doubts whether the leaks or pumps would preponderate."

Meanwhile, the Commodore's health was failing; he suffered from a severe liver ailment. Barron directed Captain John Rodgers to hoist the broad pennant on *Constitution* and assume command of the squadron.

The mission was now in the capable and agressive hands of a Truxtun-trained man, for Rodgers had been First Lieutenant of *Constellation* in the French War. The tempo of the blockade picked up almost immediately.

Constellation spent the winter of 1804-1805 on blockade duty, and also called at Tunis, Syracuse, and Malta. On March 9, 1805, Campbell requested Rodgers to release her from the blockade. The dreaded small pox had struck the crew, and thirty-two men were innoculated to prevent further spread of the disease. Rodgers would not release the ship because he wanted at least two vessels on blockade at all times. *Constellation* would have to wait.

Constitution relieved Campbell and his ship on blockade duty April 5, and Rodgers sent Campbell off to Malta, pointing out that the season for stepping up operations was approaching, and advising him to get his frigate in best possible condition for "hard Service."

Constellation called at Malta April 10, and sent a message from quarantine to Commodore Barron ashore, reporting that she had met a number of vessels about Linosa and Lampedusa, that Tripoli was building two vessels, and that a Tripolitan cruiser was at Tunis. By this time the crew had nearly all recovered from small pox with only one death.

In his report to Navy Secretary Smith dated April 11, Captain Campbell noted that he had just returned to Malta after seven weeks on the blockade. He also complained of *Constellation's* leaky condition and said he thought heaving down or docking would be necessary to get at the leaks. She had lost much copper from her bottom, with resulting in the exposure of the seams, "in which, I presume, the oakum is not very sound." Her upper works were in pretty good condition but the bottom should be repaired before "leaving these seas." Campbell then went on, apologetically, to give his views on the situation: he saw no prospect of success against Tripoli unless they could procure shallow draft gunboats to get near shore and into the harbor; the only other alternative was for the frigates to stand off shore and batter the forts and walls of the city until they had expended all their ammunition, and then resume their former stations, "an unfortunate mode of arguing."

The American campaign against Tripoli, Campbell's report continued, was further complicated by events in the Kingdom of Naples, now under Napoleon's domination. "Intrigue has conquered Italy, Naples is intirely directed by French influence, in so much as to leave the Kning with little more than a name . . .Nor shall I be surprized, if the European Wars continue much longer, to find ourselves debarr'd the

Privilege of refitting our Squadron in their Ports...." Naples
had loaned the United States Navy a number of gunboats—which had enabled Preble to conduct his agressive
campaign—but now refused to renew the loan for the next
year on the pretext that the gunboats were needed at home to
protect her shores.

While Commodore Rodgers was pressing his efforts to subdue Tripoli, one of the strangest sagas in American military
history was unfolding. A squad of seven United States
Marines under the command of Marine Lieutenant Presley
Neville O'Bannon marched from near Alexandria, Egypt, on
March 6 as the nucleus of what was surely the oddest "army"
ever assembled: three hundred Arab cavalry, seven hundred
Christians (most Greek mercenaries), one midshipman as
signal officer, and a baggage train of more than one hundred
camels. The joint commanders-in-chief of this singular force
were "General" William Eaton, erstwhile American Consul of
Tunis, and Hamet Bashaw Karamanli, older brother of Yusaf
and "rightful" ruler of Tripoli. Their mission was to march
west across the North African desert, capture Derna and
defeat the Tripolitan regime.

Eaton had convinced President Jefferson that they should
overthrow Yusaf and place his brother on the throne. Hamet,
who had attempted a takeover once before, was not eager to
risk its dangers again. His ruthless brother Yusaf had killed
their eldest brother before their mother's horrified eyes, and
now held Hamet's wife and children hostage. Eaton, O'Bannon, and the marines found Hamet in Egypt and convinced
him that they could take him back to Derna and put him on
the throne of Tripoli.

Constellation's Captain Campbell, in his report of April 11,
had informed Navy Secretary Smith of Eaton's intentions.
He was not optimistic of the outcome. Unless American vessels supported the attack on Derna, Campbell expected that
they would soon hear that Eaton and his followers had been
taken prisoner.

Meanwhile, Eaton's motley army was slogging across the
Libyan desert—following a route almost identical to that of
Montgomery's victorious campaign against Rommel in 1943.

They marched almost a thousand miles across the burning, waterless sands, fighting thirst, disease, blinding sand storms, Arab mutinies—and Hamet's uncertainty—until they reached Derna. Against powerful odds, but with the fortuitous aid of the American vessels *Hornet, Nautilus,* and *Argus,* they captured the city on April 27. They then secured the city against the subsequent counter-attacks of the Bashaw's forces. The revolution was on its way to victory and Yusaf's forces were retiring in disorder when *Constellation* appeared off Derna with the news that a treaty of peace had been signed by the United States and Tripoli.

Six weeks earlier, on May 1, 1805, Tobias Lear, United States Consul General in Algiers, had written Commodore Rodgers from Malta of word (via the Danish and Spanish consuls) that the Bashaw of Tripoli wanted to make peace. Yusaf asked that the United States pay Tripoli $200,000 for peace and ransom, and surrender all Tripolitan prisoners with their property. Lear, of course, considered these terms totally inadmissable. However, it was possible that the various pressures on Tripoli might cause Yusaf to lower the price to an "acceptable" ransom. Lear did not realize how close to collapse the Bashaw's government had come.

Finally, on June 3, a treaty of peace was drawn up and signed in the captain's cabin of the *Constitution*. The final price was $60,000. Consul General Lear felt he had won a great diplomatic victory, though nothing need have been paid at all. In just two weeks there would have been an American-backed ruler of Tripoli. In a dispatch to the Secretary of State dated June 5, Colonel Lear observed:

"This, I believe, is the first instance where a peace had been concluded with any of the Barbary States on board a ship of war! I must here pay a tribute of justice to commodore Rodgers, whose conduct during the negotiations on board, was mixed with that manley firmness, and evident wish to continue the war, if it could be done with propriety, while he displayed the magnanimity of an American, in declaring that we fought not for conquest but to maintain our just rights and national dignity, as fully convinced the negoiators, that we *did not ask, but grant, peace.*"

Lear wrote Captain Rodgers that the American prisoners would not be able to get off before the afternoon of the 4th, as the celebration of their freedom had deranged "the faculties as well as dresses of many of the Sailors" and Bainbridge would not let them go aboard the frigate until they were "quite clean and in Order." The crew of the ill-fated *Philadelphia* were free after nineteen months of captivity.

Constellation was not present when the peace was signed, but she arrived that afternoon. The frigate was immediately ordered to sail to Derna and—as we have seen—take Eaton the disappointing news that a peace was signed and that he was to discontinue hostilities. The Bashaw requested permission to send a representative to Derna on *Constellation* "to see how things are there"; his emissary would not go ashore but would communicate through letters and would return when *Constellation* was ready to leave. Permission was granted and the Bashaw's "chose" embarked.

Thus, at Derna, the victorious Eaton was informed that he and some of his followers—O'Bannon and the marines, Hamet and his aides, and the surviving Christians—had to face the humiliation of sneaking on board *Constellation* and leaving their conquest behind. The abandoned followers of Hamet were outraged and infuriated. Hamet was disconsolate.

Easton was asked to display a white flag ashore when he was ready to be evacuated, but this he refused to do. It was not until 2 A.M., under cover darkness, that all were finally aboard *Constellation*. On seeing the frigate, Yusaf's troops had taken to the hills, thinking that reinforcements were arriving for Hamet. When Hamet's troops found out that they had been abandoned, they raided Eaton's encampment, stole everything that was left, and disappeared into the desert. Thus, the Americans presented Yusaf with the kingdom he had been trying to regain. Hamet Bashaw Karamanli withdrew with a pension of two hunder dollars per month for his services rendered.

The United States squadron sailed to Syracuse at the end of that month, where on June 29 Commodore Rodgers ordered Captain James Barron to convene a Court of Inquiry into Bainbridge's loss of *Philadelphia*. The Court, consisting of James Barron, Hugh G. Campbell and Stephen Decatur, met promptly and acquitted Bainbridge of any blame for loss of his frigate.

The American squadron now turned its attention to Tunis. The Bey of Tunis was adopting a very belligerent posture and threatening to declare war unless a Tunisian xebec and her two prizes, captured by the Americans in the blockade of Tripoli, were returned. Rodgers decided to make a show of force off Tunis, and, on July 7, *Constellation, Essex, Vixen,* and *Hornet* were ordered to prepare for sea and stock up with four months' stores and powder. *Constellation,* in company with *Constitution, Essex, John Adams,* and *Enterprize,* departed Syracuse July 14, and after a two-day passage, arrived in Malta where they joined *Siren, Natuilus, Enterprize,* the store ship *Franklin,* and eight gunboats.

On July 21, Midshipman John R. Sherwood was detached from *Constellation* and ordered to take charge of the Tunisian xebec and her two prizes, while Oliver Hazard Perry was shifted to *Nautilus* as her first lieutenant.

Constellation arrived in Tunis Bay on July 30. *Constitution, Essex, John Adams,* brigs *Siren, Franklin,* and *Vixen,* schooners *Nautilus* and *Enterprize,* the store ship *Franklin,* and the eight gunboats were already at anchor. *Congress* arrived next day. Commodore Rodgers sent an ultimatum to the Bey on August 2, and gave him thirty-six hours to delcare whether he wanted war or peace. The Bey answered that he had written President Jefferson July 17, and that he would make no decision until he heard from the President, with whom he had made a treaty, and not with the commodore. Rodgers held a council of war with his captains, and as he felt that the Bey was stalling, agreed to wait three days before acting. George Davis, the United States *charge d'affairs* in Tunis, advised him to wait until the Bey heard from Washington, but Davis was sent by the Bey to *Constellation* on August 10, with the request that he be transported back to the United States.

Rodgers and his men were ready to bombard Tunis. At the last possible moment a Tunisian boat pulled out, rowing madly to *Constitution,* with authority to extend the treaty. The Bey also agreed to send an ambassador to Washington to negotiate a new treaty, and he promised not to attack

American merchantmen in the Mediterranean until the ambassador reported. Tunis had surrendered without a shot fired. For Rodgers it was vindication that resolute determination—his way, Truxtun's way, Preble's way—would win the day bloodlessly.

The Tunisian problem settled, Commodore Rodgers ordered a survey of the leaky *Constellation* by three senior captains of the squadron to decide whether she was in good enough condition to stay in the Mediterranean for another year. The Survey Board met promptly, and reported two days later that she would require a complete overhaul of her bottom, with replacement of some of her copper and caulking if she were to remain on the station at all. Rodgers decided to send her home with *John Adams*.

Constellation sailed for Malta on August 21, to take on water and stores and give Captain Campbell a chance to settle his accounts with the Navy Agent. He was then to proceed to Tangier to pick up Consul Simpson's report, and there was to take command of *Essex,* swapping with Master Commandant Charles Stewart, who was to bring the veteran warship home.

At the end of September, *Constellation* finally left the Mediterranean, and after an uneventful voyage arrived off the Chesapeake on November 13. She had trouble again making her way up the Bay, brushing shoals, and finally had to have her topmasts struck before making it up to the Navy Yard at Washington, where her crew was paid off, and she was laid up in ordinary.

Secretary of the Navy Smith reported to Congress on January 28, 1806, that *Constellation* needed repairs badly, and he could not give an estimate of the cost.

The War with the Barbary States had ceased for a time. Although not all was accomplished that might have been, the American flag was respected in the Mediterranean, American vessels admired, American merchantmen safe again, and the Navy had had the experience of successful squadron and fleet action. Most of all, the Americans now knew that Truxtun's victories were no fluke. The Navy could win!

War of 1812

For the seven years that followed the war with the Barbary States, years during which the relations between the United States and Great Britain were becoming more and more strained, *Constellation* was maintained in ordinary at the Washington Navy Yard with only a caretaker crew on board. One after another, the ships that had proved their worth in the Quasi-War and in North Africa were taken out of active service, and the training of new officers and men for the Navy was almost entirely neglected. President Thomas Jefferson and his successor James Madison saw no need for a sea-going Navy. They put their trust in the construction of gunboats for the defense of the nation's coastal cities.

By the early months of 1812, it was plain that the "War Hawks" in Congress, led by Henry Clay and John C. Calhoun, intended to force a conflict with England. As representatives of a broadening frontier constituency, they were concerned not so much about British interference with American shipping, but with the opportunity to acquire vast western and northern territories at the expense of the British and the Indians. In the Naval arena, all but the most enthusiastic supporters of the gunboat theory of defense had been persuaded that if such a war was to be fought, the United States would need warships that could meet the enemy. On March 30, 1812, Congress directed "that the gun-boats then in commission should be laid up, and with those not in commission, be distributed in the several harbors of the maritime frontier most exposed to attack, where they are to be carefully kept, and used as circumstances should require." It also authorized the immediate repair and commissioning of the frigates *Constellation, Chesapeake* and *Adams.*

Since many improvements in ship design had been made in the intervening years, it was decided to add fourteen inches to *Constellation's* beam—a change which some naval historians call the first "great repair," and claim it altered her original appearance and sailing qualities to such an extent that she became, in effect, a different ship. Her new armament would consist of two long 32's, twenty-four long 18's, and eighteen 32-pounder carronades, designed to give her a reasonably good, long range throw of metal and some close-in sock, too.

Two years later the commandant of the Washington Navy Yard described the repairs of 1812:

> The frigate *Constellation,* in February 1812, was brought to the wharf, stripped down to the lower futtocks, many of which, and some of her floor timbers, replaced with new, from thence rebuilt *up* entirely new; being much improved by fourteen inches more beam at the main breadth. Her hull being finished, she was masted and careened keel out on both sides; the new copper bolts which had been driven through her bottom all ring riveted; three new metal rudder braces fixed to her stern post, and a new rudder made; new coppered, with the exception of a few strakes near the keel; her interior joiner's work all new fitted complete; had entire new water casks, gun and carronade carriages and apparatus, together with new masts, spars, rigging and cable, sails, boats and all her stores. Was completely rigged , fitted for sea, and, in the fall of the year, left the yard a better ship in every respect than when first from the stock, and still continues to be.

War was declared on June 18, 1812, but it was six months before *Constellation* was ready for sea. She was a choice ship, considered by many the best and the luckiest in the Navy. William Bainbridge was given her command as a reward for convincing—with Charles Stewart's aid—the government that American frigates could successfully combat their British counterparts and that an American Navy at sea would ease the forthcoming blockade and wreak havoc with enemy commerce.

When the eager Bainbridge laid eyes on *Constellation* at Washington Navy Yard, his heart sank. Her guns and spars were out, and her only sticks were her lower masts. He did not want to wait six months for a crack at the British, yet he began to supervise repairs and raise a crew. Visiting Boston to see his family, Bainbridge saw Captain Isaac Hull bring in *Constitution*, victor over *Guerriere* the 38-gun in the first major naval action of the war. Hull applied for a furlough, and Bainbridge, seeing his opportunity, asked for a transfer to *Constitution*. His first lieutenant on *Constellation*, Thomas Macdonough, likewise appalled at the condition of the ship, also asked to be transferred. He, too, wanted immediate action. So *Constellation* lost her two senior officers while she was still in dry dock. (Both men went on to secure two great American naval victories. Bainbridge, commanding *Constitution*, met and defeated HMS *Java*, on December 29, 1812, and brought another laurel to "Old Ironsides." Macdonough, expecting sea duty, instead found to his surprise that he was ordered to Lake Champlain to take command of American naval forces under construction on that vital water. There, almost two years later, on September 14, 1814, Macdonough defeated the British fleet and secured the northern frontier in one of the decisive naval battles in American history.)

Command of *Constellation* was given to Captain Charles Stewart. He found the vessel still unfit for the sea, and during the autumn of 1812 labored feverishly to make her ready. These preparations were interrupted briefly by a brilliant social event. On October 27, *Constellation* was the scene of a splended ball, attended by an array of dignitaries from the national capital. The guests included Secretary of State James Monroe, heads of six Cabinet departments, senators and congressmen, and Captains Hull and Morris. The strains of stately music echoed through decks more accustomed to the roar of cannon and the shrill scream of the Boatswain's pipe. "Action," "Success," and "Victory" were the toasts of the evening. However, unknown to the assembled guests, an overwhelmingly powerful British squadron—four ships-of-the-line and four frigates–was at that very moment closing in. The nation's capital was in imminent danger of blockade.

At the time *Constellation* was being readied for war, re-inforcements for the two squadrons of the Royal Navy already in American waters were on their way. Although it meant weakening her naval forces in Europe, England had to meet the challenge for the control of the seas, and proposed to do it by sending a force to blockade the ports of the eastern seaboard of the United States. In January, 1813, a British squadron was already at the entrance to Chesapeake Bay.

Knowing that he would, in all probability, meet one or more English warships before he was far beyond the Virginia capes, Captain Stewart took advantage of the slow cruise down the bay to bring his crew to the highest state of discipline. Every evolution that a man-of-war might be called upon to carry out during battle was carefully rehearsed, and the gunners were kept busy with long drills at the great guns and at target practice. With Cape Henry in sight he dropped anchor for the night in Hampton Roads, preparing to slip out to sea the next morning.

Before she could weight anchor, the British fleet, con-sisting of line-of-battle ships, frigates, sloops, and cutters under the command of Admiral Sir John Warren and Rear Admiral Sir George Cockburn, hove in sight off Willoughby's Point and Captain Stewart was trapped. Fortunately for *Con-stellation,* the wind dropped before the British warships could get in range.

Captain Stewart had his frigate kedged up toward Norfolk until she grounded on the mud flats. When the tide refloated her that night she was carried up to the city and anchored between the two forts on the waterfront. This action blocked the further advance of the British squadron into the Roads for the time being, and when *Constellation* dropped down abreast Craney Island a few days later, she was able to de-fend the erection of further fortification on that strategic point.

Exposed as he was to attack by the British, who were lying little more than a cannon-shot away from the island, Captain Stewart kept his crew almost constantly at quarters, exercis-ing the men hour after hour at gunnery drill. As soon as dusk began to fall, he set out a flotilla of guard boats. *Constella-*

tion's lower gun ports were kept closed, and her boarding nets, boiled in half-made pitch until they were as hard as steel cables, were triced outboard toward the yardarms and loaded with kentledge (iron ballast) to fall on attacking boats when the tricing lines were cut. As a final preparation for the defense of his ship, Stewart ordered the carronades on the spar deck loaded with musket balls and their muzzles depressed so they could sweep the water near the frigate.

That these precautions were well taken soon became apparent. The British admiral, tempted by an American frigate so close at hand, attempted to approach her under cover of darkness with a fleet of small boats. Stewart's guard boats were alert, and on each occasion the alarm was given and the would-be boarders turned back without venturing to make an attack.

Captain Stewart, however, did not care for static defense. He was a deep water sailor, not a coast artilleryman. President Madison, grateful for his advice to send the Navy to sea, ordered him to Boston to relieve Bainbridge in command of *Constitution,* which he took over on June 7, 1813.

The command of *Constellation* was given Master Commandant Joseph Tarbell, a knowledgeable fighter. While continuing his predecessor's precautions, he attempted to gain the initiative and bolster the fast-sinking morale of his men by leading a flotilla of gunboats against the British frigate *Juno,* although *Barossa* and *Laurestinus* were lying close by. The gunboats, while still at long range, came to anchor and were promptly swung around by the current so that their guns could not be brought to bear. Getting under way again, they approached *Juno,* which fired several hasty and poorly aimed volleys. *Barossa* decided to take a hand in the affair and bore down on the gunboats, firing every gun she could bring to bear and the unwieldly American flotilla was compelled to retire.

On the next day, June 20, a detachment of marines and sailors from *Constellation* rowed over to Craney Island to man its batteries, which were threatened by the guns of three British 74's, one 64, four frigates, two sloops, and three transports. Stung by Tarbell's boldness, the British admiral retaliated by sending a landing party against the island on the 22nd. Seven hundred seamen, marines, chasseurs, and soldiers of the 102nd Regiment, under the command of Captain Pechell of HMS *San Domingo,* embarked in fifteen boats to mount an amphibious attack against the fortifications. While still some seventy yards from the battery, the British launch leading the attack went aground. The American gunners withheld their fire until all the British were within point-blank range, and then opened with a withering volley that sank three of the attacking boats in water so shallow that the gunwhales remained above the surface. In the confusion, Lieutenant Tatnall, with a party from the earthworks, waded out into the water and captured the sunken boats. A few of the boats' crews threw away their arms and surrendered; others escaped in the remaining boats, which made off in disorder with a loss of ninety-one men.

Commodore John Cassin, commanding the United States' naval forces at Norfolk, sent a report of the action to Secretary of the Navy Smith. The enemy's barges, he wrote, "attempted to land in front of the island out of reach of the shot from the Gunboats. When Lieutenants Neale, Shubrick and Saunders and the sailors with Lieutenant Brachinbridge and the marines of the *Constellation* one hundred and fifty in number opened fire . . . the enemy was glad to get off, after sinking three of their largest boats, one of which was called the *Santappee,* Admiral Warren's boat, Fifty feet in length carrying seventy-five men, the greater part of the crew were lost by sinking . . . The officers of the *Constellation* fired their 18-pounders more like riflemen than Artillerists. I never saw such shooting and seriously believe they saved the island." The men of the *Constellation* thought it was easier to fight from a steady platform and behind earthworks, than taking aim on a rolling, pitching deck. As a result of this engagement, Tarbell was promoted to Captain.

The enemy had had enough of amphibious warfare and were content to let the tough frigate alone. Thus, while other vessels were winning glory, *Constellation,* a floating fort, draped with anti-boarding nets, her gun deck ports nailed shut, her spar deck batteries manned, waited out the ending of the war.

One might be tempted to say that she contributed little to the 1812 war effort, until one considers that this single thirty-eight gunner partially tied down the enemy fleet for two years. The cost to England of keeping *Constellation* out of action was stupendous; her very existence posed a threat to the British. Bainbridge and Stewart realized that the very presence of a dangerous naval force, even bottled up, would strike a serious economic blow to the British, who could not afford to let such a force threaten their mastery of the sealifeline. Each British vessel on the blockade of the Chesapeake meant one less for convoy duty, and bettered the opportunities for maurading American privateers to carry out their enormously successful depletion of the British maritime. If the United States had had a few more frigates, the war would have been won all the sooner.

Sailors pose in front of Constellation   *1884*

Small arms drill on deck

N.H. circa 1884

1893

Furling sail on board during midshipman's cruise

World Tour

When the treaty of ghent was signed in December, 1814, *Constellation* was still bottled up in the Chesapeake Bay. Meanwhile, the Barbary States had taken advantage of the United States' preoccupation with England and had renewed their raids on American commerce in the Mediterranean.

Only eight days after the Senate ratified the treaty with Great Britain, President Madison recommended a full-scale war with Algiers. Congress agreed on March 2, 1815, and it was decided to send two squadrons of warships to the Mediterranean. The first squadron, which included *Constellation,* under Captain Charles Gordon, sailed from New York in May, with the broad pennant of Commodore Stephen Decatur flying from the new 44-gun frigate *Guerriere* (built in Philadelphia and named after the British ship destroyed by *Constitution*). Besides *Guerriere,* under William Lewis, and *Constellation,* there was the 38-gun frigate *Macedonian* (a prize taken from the British by Decatur and *United States*), under Jacob Jones; two sloops of war, 18-gun *Epervier,* under Captain Downes, and 16-gun *Ontario,* under Captain Elliott; three 14-gun brigs, *Firefly,* under Lieutenant Commander Rodgers, *Spark,* under Lieutenant Commander Gamble, and *Flambeau,* under Lieutenant Commander Nicolson; and two 12-gun schooners, *Torch,* under Lieutenant Commander

Chauncey, and *Spitfire,* under Lieutenant Commander Dallas.

Commodore William Bainbridge would sail with the second squadron in July, and bring an American ship of the line, the 74-gun *Independence* into action in the Old World for the first time. Having "battleships" as well as "cruisers," the United States had suddenly become an important factor in the world balance of naval strength. Now the new nation was sending to North Africa enough guns to "blow Algiers to smithereens."

After taking on stores and water, the Decatur squadron entered the Mediterranean in the middle of June, and on the 17th, sighted a large ship to the eastward of Cape de Gata. Chase was immediately begun with *Constellation* well in the lead. The stranger was the 46-gun Algerian flagship *Mashuda,* with Admiral Reis Hammida on board—a choice prize for the ship that could take her. Captain Gordon, a gunboat veteran of Preble's attack on Tripoli, desperately wanted to capture her, having been first to see the enemy vessel. His *Constellation* gained steadily and as soon as she was within range, fired a broadside that wounded Admiral Hammida. *Mashuda* immediately changed course for the sanctuary of the neutral waters of Spain, a maneuver that brought *Mashuda* within range of *Guerriere* and *Epervier* whose raking fire swept the Algerian's decks and quickly dismasted her, cutting Reis Hammida in two. The Algerians were finished, with thirty killed and many wounded.

After taking the 22-gun Algerian brig *Estedia* two days later off Cape Palos, Decatur sailed for Algiers. The mighty American flotilla barged into the harbor on June 28, 1815, flying a flag of truce to indicate the desire for a parley. Decatur informed the Dey of the fate of his admiral and two of his ships, and of the fact that the United States had declared war on Algiers. The Dey could choose a treaty or a battle, but there was to be no more tribute from America. Furthermore, negotiations would be held on the American flagship, not in the palace, and if any Algerian ships came in sight before the ratification of the new treaty, they would be seized immediately by the Americans. Dey Omar was infuriated, and frustrated, for several vessels of his diminishing fleet were expected home momentarily.

While the Dey reconsidered, an Algerian cruiser hove into sight along the horizon and *Guerriere* closed in on the ship. Immediately, a barge pulled out from the port signaling "peace" and a unique treaty was signed. All enslaved American seamen were released without ransom and there would be no more tribute. Algiers would bully the United States no more.

The fiery Decatur, who had accomplished more in a few weeks than Morris and Barron had in years, weighed anchor and led the squadron to Tunis. There were more scores to even.

On July 26, the rampaging squadron stormed into Tunis harbor where Decatur demanded $46,000 in indemnity for American vessels and prizes taken during the War of 1812. Those ships had been handed over to the British, who had assured the Bey that Tunis need never fear the Americans. The Bey was furious, but he paid.

On to Tripoli for a clean sweep. Bashaw Yusaf handed over $25,000 in reparations and liberated ten Christian slaves. For all practical purposes Barbary piracy was brought to an end. Bainbridge's squadron would enforce a "Pax Americana" in the Mediterranean, and the disappointed British, who had used the pirates to hinder the trade of competing nations, finally grew weary of the tawdry business. A year after Bainbridge arrived in the Mediterranean, a large British fleet under the command of Lord Exmouth blasted Algiers and liberated all Christian captives. With both British and American antagonism, there would be no more taking of European and American vessels and enslavement of the crews.

Meanwhile, Bainbridge and his squadron had sailed from the States on July 18, 1815. He carried orders to add Decatur's ships to his own in order to force a "peace" with the Algerians. Bainbridge was too late. Decatur had completed the job.

Now there was little for the reinforced squadron to do but show the flag and remind the North Africans of American power. Decatur sailed home in *Guerrière* to a hero's welcome and Bainbridge returned shortly afterwards with most of the squadron. He left Captain John Shaw of *United States* as commodore, with *Constellation, Ontario* and *Erie* in support. *Java,* under Captain Perry, joined Shaw later.

With the United States at peace, *Constellation* took on the unexciting but important role of commerce protection in the Mediterranean Sea. The squadron was now commanded by Commodore Isaac Chauncey, who had led the American forces in the Lake Ontario campaign and the lake battle called "The Burlington Races." Chauncey had also served under Truxtun as the latter's executive officer in *United States.* When Captain Gordon died on September 6, 1816, Captain William Crane took command of *Constellation.*

She remained in the Mediterranean until December, 1817, when she returned to Hampton Roads, bringing home Commodore John Shaw. Captain Crane began the refitting and overhauling, much needed after two years of continuous overseas service. Commodore Shaw took over the frigate and he decided to beef up *Constellation's* armament by adding four more 18-pounders to bring her up to twenty-eight long 18's, eighteen 32-pound carronades, and two long 32's.

In May, 1819, *Constellation* was designated the the flagship of Commodore Oliver Hazard Perry, almost fifteen years to the day after he had first sailed in her in 1804. Perry was ordered to take a squadron to Venezuela for the purpose of protecting American commerce from the attacks of South American privateers. He was to attempt to arrange a trade agreement between the two countries. As *Constellation* was still undergoing repairs to her hull at the time and was not yet ready for sea, Perry sailed in the smaller *John Adams.* Captain Alexander Wadsworth was ordered to take the frigate out to join him in August. When news of Perry's death from yellow fever arrived, plans were again changed. Commodore Charles Morris hoisted his broad pennant on *Constellation,* and in company with *John Adams* sailed for South America to complete Perry's mission.

Morris's orders were to "protect the vessels of the United States against piratical cruisers, and to enforce the laws prohibiting the slave trade." In 1800, any American citizen engaging in the trade was subject to two years' imprisonment and a fine of up to two thousand dollars. The slave trade was prohibited entirely in 1808. Finally, in 1820, the trade was equated with piracy and the death sentence made applicable. An anti-slavery squadron of the United States Navy was established to cruise off the mouth of the Congo River and take slavers whenever possible. The slaves were to be returned and liberated and the crews of the navy vessels involved in the capture received a bounty of twenty-five dollars per slave.

Unfortunately, the slave trade waxed instead of waned due to the enormous profits to be made and the fact that American courts did not back up the Navy with convictions. For a long time slaves had to be found on board in order to prove participation in the trade. The first American slaver was not executed until November, 1861—after the Civil War had begun!

Having completed her tour in South American waters, the "Yankee Racehorse" returned home in April, 1820, from the Rio de la Plata, with *John Adams* right behind her. The Norfolk *Beacon* of June 5, noted with pride that the entire crew of *Constellation* reenlisted, an occurrence it believed to be "without example in the naval service of this or any other country."

Constellation's next duty took her to the Pacific where in the fall of 1820, now under the command of Captain Charles G. Ridgely, she was stationed off the coast of Peru. Joining the squadron of Commodore Charles Stewart, her onetime skipper, at Callao, she relieved *Macedonia* whose task was to protect American merchantmen from attacks by both the insurgent Peruvians and the forces of the Spanish colonial government. Peru declared her independence in 1821, but fighting still persisted. Ridgely, a veteran of Preble's squadron, could not resist getting involved in the South American wars; he used *Constellation* to transport Spanish troops and treasure, some three and one-half million dollars worth, to prevent them from falling into Chilean hands. *Constellation's* tour of South America ended in the spring of 1822.

Arriving in New York on July 31, 1822, *Constellation* was laid up in ordinary for over two years, until January 27, 1825, when Master Commandant W. B. Finch sailed her to Norfolk.

From April, 1825 through 1827, she was engaged in the Caribbean, driving the last of the pirates from those waters and intercepting slavers endeavoring to reach the southern states. There was plenty of action for the crew on the West Indies Station. The Spanish possessions were hotbeds of piracy, and slaves were pouring into Cuba to work the sugar plantations. They were transported by illegal English and New England slavers called "black birders." From this duty *Constellation* returned to Norfolk and was laid up for extensive repairs.

Her captains during this period were Commodore Lewis Warrington and Captain Melancthon B. Woolsey. The former had skipperd *Peacock* when she took *Epervier* in 1814, and was one of the best-loved officers in the Navy. The latter had been Chauncey's chief aide in the Lake Ontario campaign.

In June, 1829, Captain Alexander S. Wadsworth was ordered to fit out *Constellation* for another cruise to the Mediterranean. Leaving Norfolk for New York in July, she sailed from there on August 13, carrying the Honorable Lewis McLean and William Cabell Rives, the United States' ministers-designate to England and France, and Commodore James Biddle, who had been given the command of the Mediterranean Squadron. After leaving the diplomats at Cowes and LeHavre, *Constellation* joined the United States squadron in the Mediterranean, under Captain George C. Read, in October. She cruised with the squadron until October 5, 1831, and then sailed for home.

In the spring of 1832, she joined Commodore Biddle's squadron at Naples to enforce the payment of indemnities for depredations by vessels of that state against American commerce. After spending the summer months with Commodore Daniel T. Patterson's squadron, during which she weathered a storm that sank an 80-gun French ship-of-the-line, cholera broke out on board and forced her to return to the United States in November. Additional repair work was done on *Constellation* and, in 1825, she was ordered to make a routine curise in the Caribbean. During this three-year tour of duty, the frigate took part in the Seminole War and led Commodore Alexander J. Dallas's squadron in furnishing naval reinforcements for the garrisons at Tampa and along Florida's west coast. The commodore also commanded the ship for much of the time from 1835 through 1840.

In December, 1840, the frigate, under the command of Captain George W. Storer, was again at sea bound for Rio de Janeiro where she was to join the United States squadron at the Brazil station. On February 4, 1841, Captain Lawrence Kearny assumed command of the East Indies Squadron, transferred Storer to *Potomac,* and sailed for the Orient on *Constellation.* Off South Africa, he was joined by the frigate *Boston,* and visits were made to ports in the Dutch East Indies before proceeding to China, where American trade had been curtailed by the Opium War and the British blockade of Canton.

On his arrival at Macao in March, 1842, Captain Kearny found the British in possession of the forts at the entrance to the Canton (Chukiang) River, Amoy, and Hong Kong. The Chinese were willing to enter into negotiations with the Americans who had maintained a friendly attitude throughout the Chinese struggles with Great Britain and France. Taking *Constellation* and *Boston* up the river to the Whampoo anchorage, which was forbidden to men-of-war, the American commodore established cordial relations with the Chinese authorities, while demanding and obtaining redress from their government for outrages committed on American citizens in 1841.

After a two months' visit at Whampoo, the frigates proceeded to Hong Kong, where the British had established a base and where news of the Treaty of Nanking was received in September. Appreciating the importance of the concessions Great Britain had won in this treaty—the ceding of the island of Hong Kong and the opening of the ports of Shanghai, Ning-po, Fuchau, Amoy, and Canton to British trade—Kearny ordered copies of the document sent to Washington. He postponed his departure to take advantage of his friendly relations with the Viceroy Ke and to try for similar concessions for the United States. As a result of Captain Kearny's initiative, Caleb Cushing was sent to China in 1843, where he succeeded in negotiating a commercial treaty which was the origin of the "Open Door" Policy. At that time, however, Commodore Kearny issued the following notice:

To AMERICAN MERCHANTS AND OTHERS.

All persons having goods, merchandise, or treasures to ship from one port to another on this coast, we hereby caution against entrusting the same on board any vessel in the "opium trade" sailing under the flag of the United States of North America.

Dated on board the U.S. Frigate *Constellation*, Harbor of Amoy, coast of China, this 18th day of May AD 1843.

Meanwhile, a crisis had developed in the Sandwich (Hawaiian) Islands, and *Constellation* set sail for Honolulu in late May, 1843. Since their discovery by Captain Cook in 1778, the Islands had been subject to Western influences, including American missionaries and traders, and British mercantile interests, but rule had been in the hands of native kings. In 1839, a French force seized control briefly, but the American government, concerned about both French and British interests, recognized Hawaiian independence in 1842. *Constellation* arrived after it was learned that a British officer, Captain George Paulet of HMS *Carysfort*—apparently without the knowledge of his superiors in London—had forced King Kamehameha III to cede his government to Great Britain. Captain Kearny protested vigorously:

To His Majesty Kamehameha III.
King of the Sandwich Islands:

In the name and on behalf of the people of the United States of America and their government which, the undersigned has the honor to represent, and in order to explain clearly the information of all concerned; is issued for A Protest.

Whereas a provisional cession of the Hawaiian or Sandwich Islands was made by his Majesty Kamehameha III, king, and Kekauluohi premier thereof, unto the honorable George Paulet, commanding Her Britannic Majesty's ship *Carysfort,* (to wit) on the twenty-fifth day of February, eighteen hundred and forty-three—and whereas, the United States interests and those of their citizens resident in the aforesaid Hawaiian Islands are deeply involved in a seizure of his Majesty's government under the circumstances as well as to the act of the aforesaid king and premier acceding thereto unto protest or otherwise, to affect the interests above cited:

Now therefore be it known, that I solemnly protest against every act and measure in the premises; and do declare that from and after the date of said cession until the termination of the pending negotiations between His Majesty's envoys and the government of her Britannic majesty, I hold his majesty Kamehameha III and captain Lord George Paulet answerable for any and every act, by which a citizen of the United States, resident as aforesaid, shall be restrained in his just and undisputed rights and privileges, or who may suffer inconvenience or losses, or be forced to submit to any additional charges on imports or other revenue matters, or exactions in regard to the administration of any municipal laws whatever, enacted by the "commission" consisting of his majesty king Kamehameha III, or his deputy of the aforesaid Islands, and the right Hon. lord George Paulet, Duncan Forbes Mackay, esq. and lieut. Frere, R.N.

Given under my hand on board the U.S. ship *Constellation,* at anchor off Honolulu, Oahu, this eleventh day of July, eighteen hundred and forty-three.

Lawrence Kearny, commander in chief
of the U.S. naval force in the E. Indies.

Kamehameha was persuaded to reconsider his cessation and lodge diplomatic protests. England repudiated Paulet's actions and, in 1844, recognized the independence of Hawaii. Had it not been for American naval diplomacy and Kearny's decisive conduct, Hawaii might—by virtue of possession—have come under British rule. Little did Midshipman John C. Beaumont of *Constellation* know how important was the incident he recorded in his diary on July 31, 1843:

Pleasant weather. At 10 A.M. The Hawaiian Flag was hoisted . . . under a salute of 21 guns, and the English Flag on Fort Adams was hauled down and the Hawaiian hoisted in its place and saluted with 21 guns by the English Ships of War which was returned by Fort Adams. Dressed ship and fired a salute of 21 guns with the Hawaiian flag at the Fore, in Honor of the Restoration of King Kamehameha. Our salute was returned by Fort Adams with the same numbers.

Now came the long voyage back: She sailed around Cape Horn on February 20, 1844, and into the South Atlantic, then into the North Atlantic, and finally arrived on the Carolina Coast. Under Commodore Kearny's broad blue pennant, *Constellation* had circumnavigated the globe and logged 58,000 miles and 492 days at sea.

The worn and weary ship pointed her bow to Hampton Roads on May 1, 1844. Her sails were threadbare, her stays weakened, her forty-seven-year-old hull foul and leaky. It was time to rest, perhaps never to rise again, never to shake out the sails and catch a freshening breeze on a new adventure. Younger vessels had already gone to the wreckers and the coastal graveyards. The orders came from the Navy Department: She was to lay up in ordinary once again.

They towed her up the coast to Portsmouth. She would sit out the War with Mexico, the first campaign she had ever missed.

A New Age

ALL THE TALK WAS OF *Princeton*. The Navy had fought an internal battle with forces drawn on the side of sail and on the side of steam. Steam had conquered. Then, the paddlewheeler had tussled with the Ericsson screw propeller, and the obvious technical and military superiority of the screw ship dominated. Then, the Ericsson and Stockton swivel guns, twelve inches in calibre, nearly the biggest naval cannon in the world, buried the broadside rows of carronades. Why wait for wind? Why move the whole ship to get a gun to bear, when all you had to do was move the gun?

Thus, Robert F. Stockton built the USS *Princeton* for the United States, and she was the most modern and perhaps the most effective naval warship in her time, propelled by screw and mounting twelve 42-pounders on swivels along the center line and two 12-inch giants at the bow and stern. One gun was of John Ericsson's design, the other was of Stockton's.

In February, 1844, the proud Captain Stockton brought President Tyler, Secretary of State Upshur, Secretary of the Navy Gilmer and several congressmen aboard *Princeton* for a cruise down the Potomac. The guns designed by Stockton blew up, killing Upshur, Gilmer, several congressmen, and wounding all on deck. Despite the disaster, the screw warship and the big swivel guns were here to stay.

In response to this trend, someone in the Navy Department thought up a plan to modernize *Constellation*. Why not take the old frigate and convert her into a steamer? The proposal was to dry-dock her, raze her upper deck, add thirty feet to her length, install a steam plant along the lines of the *Princeton's*, and have Stockton take charge of the ship. On July 10, 1845 the *Baltimore Patriot* reported:

> The U.S. frigate *Constellation*, the gallant ship which won the first laurels for our infant navy, under the command of Commodore Truxtun, in 1799 and 1800, is to be metamorphosed into a steamer. Orders have been received by Commodore Wilkinson, in command of the Gosport Navy yard, to proceed immediately to make the necessary alterations for that purpose, and all hands at the navy yard were busily employed yesterday in landing her armament, &c., preparatory to her being taken into dry dock, for which she will be ready to-day. Thirty feet is to be added to her length, (which will then be 200 feet,) and she will take on board the great Stockton gun, now carried by the Princeton; also the one which has been manufactured in England to the order of the navy department. The Princeton, it is ascertained, is too small to carry, without detriment, either of those enormous engines of destruction. The Constellation was built at Baltimore, and was universally acknowledged to be the most beautiful and perfect ship of her class in the world.

U.S.F. Constellation   *circa 1899*

Many citizens were not happy over the proposed alterations. Objections were sensibly raised, pointing out the greater practicality of building steam vessels from the keel up. Under the somewhat metaphorically mixed title, "Woodman! Spare that Tree," *Nile's National Register* of July 19, 1845 editorialized:

But for the additional announcement, that our favorite frigate, the laying of whose keel we had witnessed when a boy,—whose progress in building we watched with intense interest—whose beautiful launch from her *ways,* into her destined element we witnessed in the year 1797, and can yet hear the glorious shout of the thronging thousands, that greeted her first float upon the 'mountain wave,'—whose early achievements under the command of the gallant Truxtun, were never eclipsed, even by the subsequent achievements of "OLD IRONSIDES" herself—that the CONSTELLATION was to be *razed*—cut up—cut down—*stretched out* or altered in any form or shape, from AN AMERICAN FRIGATE, to undergo the *screwing—wheeling* or *paddling* of empirics in "naval architecture"— especially of those whose capacities have been tested by such results, as the 'Peace maker' on the one hand, and the 'Princeton' on the other—have exhibited, we do most earnestly protest. If the Princeton is too small, give captain Stockton a carte blanche for building a steamer as big as he pleases—but spare what we have, of the keel and canvas, that has given our navy the character it has.—Hands off—there!

The following communication, from one who is evidently acquainted with his subject, we extract from the National Intelligence of Thursday last, as more to the purpose and better expressed than aught that we could say on the subject:

To the honorable GEORGE BANCROFT,
Secretary of the navy.

You have ordered that the United States frigate CONSTELLATION be placed in charge of captain Stockton for the purpose of having her converted into a steamer to be propelled by what some call Steven's and others Loper's propeller.

Permit me, sir, respectfully to suggest, that, previous to taking final action in this matter, you will give it full and deliberate consideration. It is an important matter; and, should it prove a failure in any respect, you may rely upon it that the people of these United States will not readily excuse an act which is to shear that herioic ship of a single branch of the laurels she so gallantly earned in the early days of our glorious title navy.

The CONSTELLATION, under the gallant TRUXTUN, gained her country one of the most brilliant victories in the annals of any navy. She is one of the naval idols of our country. Profane will be deemed the hand that may desecrate her.

Colonel Humphreys, United States Chief Naval Constructor, rode down to Norfolk to inspect *Constellation*. He saw, finally, the sheer impossibility of the project, and she was left in peace for a few years. It seemed that her active life was over, fraying to a desultory end; but *Constellation* was to be reborn again.

Seven lean years passed while *Constellation* lay in ordinary at the Gosport Navy Yard at Portsmouth. She was rotting away, literally.

Perhaps it was sentimentally inspired, for *Old Ironsides* had been reprieved by public action and the pen of Oliver Wendell Holmes, but a decision was made by the United States Bureau of Construction and Repair to modernize the ship rather than follow the current trend of destroying the vessel, building a new one under the old name, and calling it "repairs" in order to circumvent Congress's loathness to finance sorely needed new construction. The job took two years, and although the alterations were extensive, the resulting vessel was still *Constellation*. They cut her in two, aft of frame number ten and inserted a twelve-foot section into her hull. Her spar deck was stripped of its old fashioned carronades. Secretary of the Navy James C. Dobbins wanted a first class fighting sloop-of-war of 22 guns, with armament concentrated on the gun deck. He got a ship which was, according to a Norfolk newspaper, "equal in size and guns to any fighting ship on the sea."

In 1854, the Secretary of the Navy reported to Congress that "the *Constellation*, was built in 1797, as a frigate of the second class, and had been many times rebuilt. Being found altogether unworthy of further repairs, she has been rebuilt as a spar-deck sloop . . ." When she came off the ways after the work had been completed, *Constellation's* length between perpendiculars had been increased by twelve feet, her moulded beam by six inches, and her depth in hold by seven feet seven inches. Her new dimensions: length between perpendiculars, 176 feet; beam, 41 feet; depth, 21 feet, 1 inch. These alterations were made at a cost of $270,000; a new sloop would have cost the government between $350,000 and $500,000. For the men of the Navy she was still the old and glorious *Constellation.* Her weaponry now consisted of two ten-inch shell guns, sixteen eight-inch guns, and four thirty-two pounders. After sea trials, it was decided that her armament was too heavy, and the shell guns—the only pivot guns in the lot and the most effective modern weapons—were removed.

Constellation was put back into commission at Gosport on July 28, 1855, under the command of Captain Charles H. Bell, and she was ordered to join the Mediterranean Squadron off Spezia Bay on the west coast of Italy. After taking on stores and supplies for a long cruise, she sailed from Norfolk. The tour of duty in the Mediterranean was uneventful; she was detached from the squadron at Genoa on April 17, 1858, hoisted her homeward-bound pennant, and sailed for New York. She came to anchor in the East River on June 5, having sailed 29,227 miles since leaving the United States three years before. Now came orders for a brief cruise to Cuban waters, then back to New York where, on August 13, 1858, she was taken out of commission at the Brooklyn Navy Yard.

In June, 1859, *Constellation* was recommissioned at Boston and, under the command of Captain John S. Nicholas, sailed for the west coast of Africa. There she acted as flagship of a squadron under Captain William Inman that was engaged in breaking up the slave trade from the Congo region. She took up her station off the Congo River on November 21, 1859. Her crew suffered from the intolerable heat and the ever-present fever.

The Anglo-American effort to put down the infamous international slave trade had gone on for two generations, though unsupported by the courts of the United States or by Congresses and Parliaments. It is to the everlasting credit of these navies that they wholeheartedly attempted to destroy the pernicious and cancerous trade, just as it is to the everlasting shame of the governments they served that support for this humanitarian work was at best half-hearted. Many of the African and Arab leaders sold blacks, (sometimes their own people), to the European "factors" who wholesaled to the trade, to transporters, to the Brazilizan, Cuban, and Southern American importers and smugglers.

But the worst villains were the New England "black-birders" who crammed tiny ships with chained human cargo and left them to rot in their own filth for the entire voyage, jettisoning the dead, and selling the pitiful survivors for enormous profits.

The slaves were branded ashore and flogged aboard. On British slavers, generally larger vessels, the women were permitted to roam the decks and given the "privilege" of slaking the lusts of the crew. If a girl resisted she would be smashed by fist or whip into submission. The men were jammed below decks in chains, and dragged up on the weather deck once a day to perform a grotesque dance believed to be beneficial to the health of the slaves. Food was usually a minimal quantity of rice or yams or corn mush, which if refused by a slave, would be forced down his mouth.

The squadron commodore, William Inman, used the new title "flag officer." Like commodore, it referred to a captain in command of a squadron, and the title would be his, as was the custom, for the rest of his life. Inman was not an energetic man. He was an old salt whose service dated back to the War of 1812. A New Jersey man, he was given command of one of the largest peacetime squadrons in American history to that date, because Secretary of the Navy Isaac Touchey was determined to suppress the trade. After all, the African Station had been manned for sixteen years by American warships, and the slave traders had not declined but increased in number. Inman had twice as many ships as any previous commodore. In addition to his flagship *Constellation*, there were seven vessels: *San Jacinto* and *Portsmouth*, both first class sloops; two second class sloops, *Mohican* and *Vincennes;* the third class steamers *Mystic* and *Sumpter;* and *Marion*, a third class sloop.

Despite the strength at his command, Inman had little success initially. But at last *Constellation* made a capture. She took the slave brig *Delicia* on December 21, 1859, off Kabenda. Secretary Touchey ordered Inman to persevere.

Then a stroke of good luck turned an ineffectual patrol into one of the great slave liberations accomplished by the United States Navy. *Mohican* and *San Jacinto* converged west of

Kabenda on August 8, 1860, and found two almost becalmed vessels, *Erie* and *Storm King,* both slavers. The *Mohican* prepared for action. *Erie* had to be a blackbirder. The warship fired a warning shot and *Erie* hove to and was boarded by *Mohican's* search detachment. The crew of the slaver surrendered without a shot, and the Navy rescued 900 chained blacks. Meanwhile, *San Jacinto* overhauled *Storm King* and discovered 180 women, 164 men, 68 girls and 261 boys enslaved aboard the brig. All of the captives were taken to Monrovia for liberation, while their captors and the slave ships were sent home for trial and confiscation.

The squadron had accomplished something at last. Now it was *Constellation's* turn once more. During the evening of September 26, the lookouts spotted a vessel that looked suspicious. By the light of the moon, the sloop took up the chase. The unidentified vessel chose to flee and began to hurl her moveables overboard to lighten ship. The moonlit sea was littered with casks, spars, boats and hatches as *Constellation* knifed through the jetsam. Captain Nicholas ordered warning blanks fired but to no avail. The eight-inchers opened up with live ammunition, firing high on purpose. At 11 P.M., the slaver gave up. She was the bark *Cora,* loaded with 705 Africans. They were sent to Monrovia.

The Civil War had commenced with the attack on Fort Sumter, April 12, 1861, but *Constellation* would not learn of this for many months. On May 21, 1861, whe sighted a brig, apparently American and very likely a slaver. She was flying a set of colors which Captain Nicholas could not locate in his signal book; in fact, the flag at the gaff looked like a Revolutionary War flag. Not one to take chances, but not wanting to lose a slaver, Nicholas sent a round shot blazing across the brig's bow. She hove to and proved to be the American slaver *Triton* out of Charleston, South Carolina. *Constellation* had made the first official capture of the Civil War.

Nicholas placed a prize crew aboard the brig with orders to sail her to Norfolk, but they found that city in Confederate hands, and took her to New York. Meanwhile, *Constellation* remained in African waters through most of the summer of 1861, her tour uneventful except for the severe illness of Captain Nicholas. He was dispatched home in June, and Captain Thomas A. Dorin relieved him in command. On August 11, *Constellation* left Africa waters and sailed out of sight of "Station Misery." An exhausted and feverish crew brought the sloop to anchor at Portsmouth, New Hampshire, on September 28, 1861.

Much of the navy had been put to the torch at Norfolk, and by this time much of the countryside itself was in flames. The homecoming was not a joyous one, and *Constellation* would have to gird herself for that most terrible of conflicts, war with one's own countrymen.

Early in 1862, The United States Navy was in the process of rebuilding, after mass defection of Southern-born officers and men and the loss of many ships at the burning of the Norfolk Navy Yard. Four hundred merchant ships were impressed into the fleet, and every available war vessel was sent out on assignment. Work immediately commenced to make *Constellation* ready for sea again. Once more her armament was changed and brought up to date, making use of the best naval guns available.

Captain Henry K. Thatcher, who had once served on *Constellation* as a midshipman, was given her command. On March 10, 1862, Secretary Welles wrote him:

> The main object in sending the *Constellation* to the Mediterranean is the protection of our commerce from the practical depredations of the vessels fitted out by those in rebellion against the United States. The principal one of these vessels, the *Sumter*, which has so far eluded our cruisers, when last heard from was in the vicinity of Gibraltar. Your chief duty will be the pursuit of that vessel, should she remain in that quarter. At the same time, however, you will exercise vigilance in all cases.

It was a pipe dream to expect an old sailing ship to catch and destroy a steam blockade runner. For two fruitless, almost pathetic years, Thatcher and the weary crew of *Constellation* chased one Rebel raider after another but to no avail. In July, 1863, Thatcher was relieved by Captain Henry S. Stellwagen, and the next summer found *Constellation* off Tunis again, protecting American property and citizens as that city-state underwent yet another revolution.

Recalled from the Mediterranean, *Constellation* reported to Rear Admiral David Glasgow Farragut at New Orleans. She was considered for service to the West Gulf Blockading Squadron, but she drew too much water for close inshore work. Furthermore, her lack of auxiliary steam power precluded her use in confined waters. Despite this, Farragut immediately sent her to a patrol station between Galveston and Havana.

On December 14, *Constellation* beat her way into Havana harbor and anchored. The neutral port was swarming with Confederate shipping. With a shrug of his shoulders, Stellwagen gave his men liberty anyway. *Constellation* bluejackets rushed ashore and into the midst of their Rebel counterparts. They were Americans all.

The skipper had remained on board. Slowly, on shaky legs, the first liberty party returned. Some men were so drunk they had to be hoisted over the side. The officer of the watch ordered the inebriates sluiced down with cold water. Stellwagen decided to come up on deck to deliver a temperance lecture. As he strode onto the deck, he was shocked to see many of his men were wearing Confederate uniforms. They had swapped **hats and blouses** with their Southern drinking companions.

Stellwagen did not wait for any of the Confederate steamers to leave the port—he could not have caught them anyway. He proceeded to take *Constellation* back to Farragut, now off Mobile. The old admiral must have sighed to see her. As a young lieutenant, he too had walked her decks, but now she was of little use to him. He wanted iron and speed, not wood and beauty. Farragut sent *Constellation* to Norfolk, now back in Union hands, to discharge her crew. Stellwagen tried to recruit a new crew, but it was almost impossible. Every able-bodied seafarer was already in the service. Thus, *Constellation* was assigned as a recruit training vessel, and her "boots" went out into the fleet to man the various squadrons bombarding and throttling the last Southern ports.

Captain Stellwagen was relieved on January 19, 1865, by Captain J. de Camp, who held the dockside command as the war ended. In November of that year Commander Albert G. Clary took over the ship. The following June, the steamer

Miles Standish towed *Constellation* up to Philadelphia where she became one of the many old wooden receiving ships. Recruits and drafts came and went. *Constellation* became more and more like a barracks and less like a fighting ship. On June 26, 1866, Commander William Rockendorf assumed command of the vessel for a year, until Captain de Camp was ordered to take her out of commission. Later in 1869, *Constellation* was towed to Norfolk for much needed repairs.

Until the War with Spain, *Constellation* was always on call to perform special missions: training, showing the flag, good will tours, relief and diplomatic missions. Early in 1871, the Navy decided to use her as a training vessel for midshipmen at Annapolis, and on May 25, the old racehorse was back in harness under Captain Samuel P. Carter and cruising along the New England coast. Her next skipper was Captain William N. Jeffers, who took command on October 18, and promptly ran the ship aground twice on the short voyage from Annapolis to Washington. *Constellation* never did like that little trip. She finally made it to the Washington Navy Yard on November 9, where she remained until the following February, when the Navy Department put her to use as a gunnery practice ship.

Constellation sailed to the Naval Academy for a load of midshipmen on June 5, 1872 and took them for a practice cruise until September 30. The winter of 1872 was spent riding at anchor off Annapolis. On April 10, 1873, Captain Jeffers was relieved by Lieutenant Commander William R. Bridgeman, who held command only a few weeks until the arrival of Commander Augustus P. Cooke in May. *Constellation* departed Annapolis early in June, for another midshipman training cruise. She returned September 29, and proceeded to Norfolk where she was temporarily placed out of commission in October.

For several years, *Constellation* would be used as a summer training ship, and then be laid up each winter. Recommissioned on May 16, 1874, her new skipper, Commander K. R. Breese, took the midshipmen on the next summer cruise, returning in September to be relieved by Lieutenant Commander P. F. Harrington, who placed the vessel out of commission again at Norfolk. It was back to the training wars the following summer under Commander Edward Terry and then a year and a half out of commission. On May 31, 1875, Terry sailed up to Annapolis, loaded another group of future admirals and captains-the naval officers of the War with Spain and World War I-and headed south. In September she was back in Norfolk and out of commission.

She finally received a more challenging assignment. On March 13, 1878, Captain James A Greer sailed for New York to load the American exhibits which would be shown at the Paris Exhibition that year. *Constellation* was to be accompanied by *Constitution*. These two historic ships, each nearly one hundred years old, sailed to Le Havre in April. There, they unloaded cargo. Turning about, *Constellation* proceeded to Annapolis to embark yet another training crew. Captain Greer was relieved by Commander H. L. Howison on July 24, 1878, and two days later traveled south. Back home in September, she was out of commission again.

In 1879, a real attempt was made to keep her a useful, active vessel. The summer found her once more on a training cruise with Commander Frederick V. McNair in charge. When *Constellation* returned in September, she was temporarily placed out of commission until November 10, when Captain Henry Wilson loaded her with men and supplies for the flagship of the Mediterranean Squadron and sailed eastward. At Gibraltar on December 10, *Constellation* transferred men and cargo to the USS *Trenton*, squadron flagship, and Captain Wilson exchanged billets with the *Trenton* skipper, Captain John L. Davis, who brought the vessel back to New York on January 20, 1880.

In March, 1880, Commander Edward E. Potter took over. The ship was loaded with foodstuffs for the relief of famine-stricken Ireland. The supplies were made available as a result of the efforts of the *New York Herald's* Irish Relief Fund drive. On March 30, she departed for Queenstown, Ireland, arriving at that port on April 20, where she was met by British vessels to implement the distribution. She remained at Queenstown until May. On her way home she sailed by a road of vessels carting immigrants to the United States.

U.S.F. Constellation *loading supplies for Ireland at the Brooklyn Navy Yard   March, 1880*

The next thirteen years, *Constellation* spent training midshipmen in the summer and lying idle in the winter. It was not exciting for ship or crew, but at least she was active. The Navy had turned to steam and steel. Alfred Thayer Mahan was creating new concepts of sea power; the United States was just beginning to realize the necessity for a large modern fleet, a two-ocean navy, and a canal across the Isthmus of Panama (to allow the fleets to move more quickly from one coast to another). Still, future naval officers could best learn the ancient craft of seamanship and the traditions of a great service on a ship such as *Constellation*. One could study the steam cycle, modern damage control, and high powdered gunnery a little later on perhaps. Pride in country, courage, and confidence came first—and these lived in the oak heart of *Constellation*.

On September 6, 1892, Commander Caspar F. Goodrich assumed command and, after supervising a month of much needed repairs, he sailed her across the Atlantic to Naples. Another interesting assignment now fell to *Constellation*. Her mission was to carry works of art from Italy and France for exhibition at the World Columbian Exposition. It was due to open at Chicago in May, 1893, in celebration of the 400th, anniversary–one year late of the discovery of America. More paintings and sculptures were carefully stored on board at Le Havre, and by mid-January Goodrich and his ship of art treasures were en route to New York.

In February, the precious cargo was unloaded and *Constellation* proceeded to Norfolk for more repairs. In the summer of 1893, under Commander W. Chester, *Constellation* made her last training cruise. Some of the young men who sailed as midshipmen on her would become high ranking naval officers in the next century.

On September 25, 1893, while out of commission, the ship was towed to Norfolk from Annapolis. There she was patched up again and taken in tow to Newport, Rhode Island. She arrived on May 22, 1894, and served as a receiving ship in which recruits and men in transit would be temporarily berthed. Thus, for the next twenty years, *Constellation* was employed serving her country in her own small way.

Trainees aloft at Newport, R.I. training station

circa 1912

Into the 20th Century

The Centennial Celebration of the Star Spangled Banner, held in Baltimore in September, 1914, renewed interest in the old ship. Assistant Secretary of the Navy Franklin D. Roosevelt, who had made an extensive study of the early Navy, took a keen interest in the refitting of *Constellation* for the Centennial. Later, in a detailed report to Secretary of the Navy Josephus Daniels, Roosevelt wrote: "She is longer and she is a sloop, but she is still the same clipper type *Constellation.*"

On June 17, 1914, commanded by Captain Roger Wells, she was towed by the *Uncap* to Norfolk where she was stripped of her modern equipment and restored to her original appearance (as much as possible). Proceeding to Baltimore on September 3, *Constellation* was the center of interest when on September 9, a tablet was unveiled on the famous ship to commemorate her return to the city and to officially inaugurate the Centennial's program. She returned to Norfolk for the winter, and in the spring of 1915 she resumed her duties as a training ship at Newport.

On October 30, 1917, her name was officially changed to *"Old Constellation"* when a modern battle cruiser was named *Constellation.* This upstart was, however, a victim of the Arms Limitation Treaty and was scrapped in accordance with the terms of that agreement in 1922. So, on July 24, 1925, the name of the old ship was officially restored.

Constellation made another voyage from the sheltered waters of Narrangansett Bay in May, 1926, when she was towed south for the Philadelphia Sesqui-centennial Exposition. Hailed as the oldest vessel in the United States Navy, she was manned by a crew of twenty-eight men from the honor company at the Newport Naval Training Station—under the command of Chief Boatswain E. D. Delazy. With flags flying and bands playing, she tied up in Philadelphia where she attracted thousands of visitors. On her return to Newport, *Constellation* was maintained as an exhibit open to the public until November, 1939.

Still, *Constellation* was not quite ready for retirement. When the opening guns of World War II were fired, it did not seem possible that a warship whose muzzle-loading guns and flaxen sails had long since been replaced by long range breech-loading rifles and steam would be called upon to take part in the cataclysm that was to follow.

As President Washington had warned Congress in 1796, nations at war have little respect for neutrals who the lack naval and military forces to punish those who violate their rights. The experiences of the United States in World War I had demonstrated the necessity of a strong navy to protect its commerce against submarine and surface raiders. By the early months of 1940, a program of expansion for the Navy was well underway, but was seriously hampered by a lack of training facilities. *Constellation* was once more pressed into service to house and train the Sea Unit, which was made up of graduates of the Newport Naval Training Station's "boot" courses. These graduates required further specialized training before being sent to sea. On August 24, 1940, the ship was placed in full commission by order of President Roosevelt, who thought that the service of a vessel whose glorious career paralleled as well as personified the growing strength and the continuing valor of the American nation would serve to remind the American people and the world of the long naval tradition of maintaining the freedom of the seas. It was a dramatic revival for a vessel Roosevelt called "a ship of

destiny." One of the Navy's most picturesque officers,
Lieutenant Commander John Davis, was called back from
retirement and given command of the ship.

*Active duty again. Sailors holystone the deck
Newport, R.I. November, 1939*

On deck, Vice Adm. Ingersoll and Rear Adm. Hustvedt during WWII. Photo: Barrett Gallagher, USN.

U.S.F. Constellation *as she appeared in February, 1942*

Under this energetic officer, *Constellation* again resumed active duty. A thorough inspection was made, rotted timbers were replaced, and the ship's interior arrangements were altered to adapt her to her new role. As a final touch, Davis had the bilges cleaned of several feet of mud that had accumulated over the years, and he had the cast iron ingots that were used for ballast carried on deck to be scrubbed and painted.

On May 20, 1941, *Constellation* was designated the relief flagship of Admiral Ernest J. King, Commander-in-Chief, United States Atlantic Fleet. Extensive changes were made in the below-decks spaces to accommodate the complex modern radio equipment that was necessary for a ship that was the nerve-center of the anti-submarine war in the Atlantic Ocean.

"The Day of Infamy" came and most of the major warships of the Atlantic Fleet were transferred to the Pacific to make up for the losses at Pearl Harbor. On January 19, 1942, *Constellation* was assigned duty as flagship of Vice Admiral Royal E. Ingersoll, Commander-in-Chief, United States Atlantic Fleet, and later that year she became the flagship of Rear Admiral C. F. Bryant, Commander of Battleship Division 5 of the Atlantic Fleet. She continued on active duty until the end of hositilities in Europe and with Japan. This assignment was a fitting climax to her long years of service.

In 1947, *Constellation* was taken to the Boston Naval Shipyard for final disposition. Some felt that she was beyond repair. A handful of patriotic men who felt that a ship with such a glorious history and tradition should not be allowed to die, saved her from being scrapped. Congress passed a bill in 1949, providing for her restoration if seventy-five per cent of the estimated cost of $4,525,000, could be raised by the public. However, interest faltered and the movement died with less than one hundred dollars having been pledged.

Moored to a pier near the more fortunate *Constitution, Constellation* was rapidly deteriorating and prompt action was required if she was to be saved. By 1951, her old masts were so frail that they had to be removed, and much of the caulking about her beautifully carved stern and forepeak was lost.

In Boston alongside "Old Ironsides"

October, 1947

In Boston — deck view looking forward

The exposed woodwork gave way to dry rot, but the great oaken knees that supported the weight of her gun deck and its artillery, and much of the internal planking remained relatively sound. Most of her frame and furnishings could be left in place if she were restored.

A second surge of interest in the old ship occurred in 1953, but the drive for contributions was little more successful than the abortive appeal four years earlier, and the Navy Department requested permission to scuttle her. Fortunately, the Congressional committee that had cognizance of the matter tabled the proposal, and the fight to save her was taken up the the Star Spangled Banner Flag House Association of Baltimore, a patriotic, non-profit organization of private citizens. The Association asked the Navy to tow the ship to Baltimore in a floating dry dock while its members undertook to raise the funds necessary to restore her. As the Navy Department lacked an appropriation to meet the expense of this proposal, estimated at $15,000, no action was taken.

In 1954, Congress passed a bill authorizing the Navy to move *Constellation* to Baltimore, and turn her over to the Flag House Association for restoration. During the following summer, the old ship was fitted with a temporary mast which was strung with Navy code flags spelling "Yankee Race Horse," and she was placed in a seagoing dry dock. A powerful tug towed the dry dock from Boston to the Chesapeake Bay. *Constellation* succeeded in reaching the sheltered waters of the Patapsco River just a few days before a disastrous hurricane struck the Atlantic seaboard. The fact that she made port ahead of the hurricane (which would almost certainly have ended her career if it had caught her at sea) was regarded by her well-wishers as a happy omen of new life. She was 158 years old.

In 1955, the Constellation Committee of Maryland was formed. On September 7, 1957, her 160th birthday was celebrated at her mooring at Pier 4, Pratt Street, Baltimore, with ceremonies appropriate to her return home. The Committee set out to raise funds to restore their heirloom and to find her a permanent berth.

Constellation *at her lowest point before restoration.*

A Great Ship returns home

The task was complicated by a controversy over the ship's authenticity. There were some who maintained that the rebuilding in 1853, which altered her dimensions and converted her from a frigate to a sloop, marked the end of the *Constellation* that had been launched in 1797. They argued that she was virtually a new ship, but the Navy Department steadfastly maintained that alterations in the lines and structure of a ship do not make a new ship, and that the vessel now in Baltimore is the *Constellation*. In 1957, Rear Admiral E. M. Eller, Director of Naval History in the office of the Chief of Naval Operations, wrote that there "is not now and has not been any change in the Navy's pride in the *Constellation* as one of our most historic ships continuously on the Navy rolls since she first went to sea in 1798." Admiral Eller stated that nowhere in the records of the Navy Department was there any indication that the original *Constellation* was "broken up, stranded, scrapped or otherwise disposed of." She, in fact, retains about 30% of her original materials.

Night work on Constellation *at Maryland Shipbuilding & Drydock*

The task of restoring the ship to her 1812 appearance was begun finally. In 1964, *Constellation* had her first major overhaul at Maryland Shipbuilding & Drydock Company, with most of the repair work being concentrated above the waterline. A new bowsprit was fitted, and masts and yards were replaced or rebuilt. New gun ports were cut in her spar deck bulwarks to reconvert her from a sloop-of-war to a frigate. In 1971, she spent three days at Maryland Drydock having her hull painted.

In August, 1972, *Constellation* was moved to her mooring in Baltimore's Inner Harbor, where, on September 7, 1973, she celebrated the 175th anniversary of her launching. The United States Congress officially recognized this occasion by authorizing special silver and bronze medals that were struck by the Philadelphia Mint. Replica guns and gun mounts were completed for the ship in time to celebrate the Nation's bicentennial in 1976; *Constellation* was designated official flagship for the year-long festivities.

The effort to keep *Constellation* afloat continues. Most recently, she underwent a below-the-waterline overhaul which was financed by the State of Maryland for one and a half million dollars. Repairs were carried out at Bethlehem Steel Corporation's Fort McHenry dry dock in Baltimore, from November, 1979, through July, 1980. In the following year, she returned to the shipyard for work above the waterline. This was made possible by a $600,000 grant from the National Trust for Historic Preservation and paid through the Maryland Historic Trust. From there, she returned to her berth at Pier 1, in the Inner Harbor, where she is open to the public year-round.

Constellation served the United States and her Navy proudly, as warship, training ship, and flagship, for 150 years. She continues to serve today, as a living symbol of the values—patriotism, pride, and honor—which built a Navy and strengthened a young republic.

How shall we sum up a century and a half of service? How do we bridge the vast chasm of technology that yawns between the eighteenth century and our own time? In retrospect, it seems that theirs was an innocent time, a romantic time. We might easily take as its symbol the Yankee frigate, one of the most complicated machines ever devised by man, driven by the capricious power of the wind, and manipulated by the puny strength of human beings, and yet, when under full sail on a foam-flecked emerald sea, flying like a beautiful white dove, truly the stateliest of ships.

"Ship ahoy! What ship is that?"

CONSTELLATION

Glossary

ABEAM: On a line at right angles to the ship's keel; opposite the middle of the ship's side.

AFT (ABAFT): In or toward the stern of the ship.

BEAR UP: To alter the ship's course so that she runs with the wind.

BEAT UP: To make progress to windward by tacking.

BRIG: A two-masted vessel, square-rigged on masts of nearly equal height.

BROADSIDE: The entire discharge of all guns on one side of the ship.

CARRONADE: A short, iron cannon.

CORSAIR: A Mediterranean privateer.

GRAPESHOT: A cluster of small iron balls used as a cannon charge.

GUNBOAT: A small, light, shallow-draft vessel usually carrying only one gun.

HOVE TO: Trimming the sails so that the ship is making no headway; stopped.

HULLED: Shot in the hull at point-blank range.

KEDGE: A small anchor; To move a vessel by carrying a kedge in a boat, dropping it overboard, and hauling the vessel up to it.

KEEL: A longitudinal timber or series of timbers extending along the center of the bottom of the vessel.

LARBOARD: The left-hand side of the ship as one faces the bow.

LEEWARD: The side of the ship that is sheltered from the wind.

MAN-OF-WAR: A war vessel of a recognized navy armed for active hostilities.

MERCHANTMAN: A trading vessel.

MOLE: A stone structure which is a breakwater and a mooring space for ships on the shore side.

PRIVATEER: An armed vessel commissioned to cruise against the merchantmen or warships of an enemy.

ROADSTEAD: A protected place where ships may ride at anchor.

SCHOONER: A fore- and aft-rigged vessel having two or more masts.

SHIP-OF-THE-LINE: A sailing battleship having two or three full gun decks mounting 64, 74, or 80 guns.

SLOOP: A single-masted vessel carrying a large mainsail and a single head sail.

SPOKE: Communication with another vessel.

STARBOARD: The right-hand side of the ship as one faces the bow.

TATTOO: A call on a drum notifying the sailors to repair to quarters.

WEAR AROUND: To put the ship on the other tack by turning her away from the wind.

XEBEC: A small craft native to the Barbary pirates.

YARD: A long piece of timber suspended across a mast to spread a sail to the wind.

A Selected Bibliography

Allen, Gardner W. *Our Navy and the Barbary Corsairs.* Hamden, Connecticut [1905], 1965.

Braisted, William Reynolds. *The United States Navy in the Pacific.* Austin, Texas, 1958.

Chapelle, Howard I. *The History of the American Sailing Navy.* New York, 1949;
  The History of American Sailing Ships. New York, 1935.

Dawson, Henry B. *Battles of the United States by Land and Sea.* New York, 1858.

DeConde, Alexander. *The Quasi-War.* New York, 1966.

Dorset, Phyllis Flanders. *Historic Ships Afloat.* New York, 1967.

Dugan, James. *The Great Mutiny.* New York, 1965.

Ferguson, Eugene S. *Truxtun of the Constellation.* Baltimore, 1956.

Herrick, Walter R., Jr. *The American Naval Revolution.* Baton Rouge, Louisiana, 1966.

Knox, Dudley W. "Documents on the Naval War with France," *United States Naval Institute Proceedings,* LXI (April 1935), 535-538;
  History of the United States Navy. New York, 1936.

Laing, Alexander. *American Sail.* New York, 1961.

Naval Documents Related to the Quasi-War between the United States and France, 1797-1801. 7 volumes. United States Naval Records and Library Office. Washington, D.C., 1935-1938.

Naval Documents Related to the United States Wars with the Barbary Powers, 1785-1807. 7 volumes. United States Naval Records and Library Office. Washington, D.C., 1939-1945. (Volume 7 is *Register of Officer Personnel...and Ships' Data,* 1801-1807.)

Pope-Hennessy, James. *Sins of the Fathers.* New York, 1968.

Pratt, Fletcher. *Preble's Boys.* New York, 1950;
  The Navy: A History. Garden City, New York, 1941.

Tucker, Glenn. *Dawn Like Thunder.* Indianapolis, 1963;
  Poltroons and Patriots. 2 volumes. Indianapolis, 1954.

Acknowledgements and Credits

Photographs on pages, 7, 15, 59, 61, 86, 150, 165, 168, 169, 171, 172, 173, 174, 175, 177, 178, 179, 180 courtesy of U.S.F. Constellation Foundation, Inc.

Photographs on pages 18, 99, 138, 160, 162, 166, courtesy of U.S. Department of the Navy.

Maps on inside cover and on page 117 courtesy of U.S. Department of the Navy.

Photograph on page 77 from an original painting by Arthur N. Disney, Sr.

Photographs on pages 136 and 137: Patch Collection, Strawbery Banke, Inc. of Portsmouth, New Hampshire.

Index